"Churches are suddenly . . . . their communities have
changed ethnically, economically, and culturally and the church no longer reflects the community. *re:MIX—Transitioning Your Church to Living Color* com-
bines a solid biblical-theological base, case studies, as well as a practical guide
to becoming a healthy multiethnic church. I highly recommend this book for
local churches, denominational leaders, and lay people. It is a MUST read and
practice for the future of the church."
—Jo Anne Lyon, General Superintendent, The Wesleyan Church

"There are a lot of people who can point you to the city on the hill, but very few
can give you a road map on how to get there. I am hearing more than ever about
the need for multiethnic churches, but when the question is *How?* the conversation gets stuck—until now. DeYmaz and Whitesel have produced a masterful
work on principles and practices in becoming a multiethnic church. These men
are not just theorists but have been in the trenches doing the work. If you are
serious about your church looking like the kingdom of Heaven in Revelation
7:9 then this is a must-read book."
—Rodney L. Cooper, PhD, Kenneth and Jean Hansen Chair of Discipleship
and Leadership, Gordon-Conwell Theological Seminary, Charlotte, NC

"*re:MIX—Transitioning Your Church to Living Color* is a timely book. The
United States is becoming a majority-minority nation with no single prominent
majority ethnicity, and local churches must become more sensitive and hospi-
table, embracing multiculturalism. While the gospel is transcultural, DeYmaz
and Whitesel show convincingly that the proclamation and incarnation of the
gospel must be decidedly and intentionally multicultural, reflecting and affirm-
ing the vast diversity of the body of Christ. This book shows how theory and
practice can work hand-in-hand in creating 'churches of living color,' and the
authors provide real-world examples and suggestions for responding to the clar-
ion call of God to love him by loving the diverse world he created."
—James R. Hart, President, Robert E. Webber Institute for Worship Studies

"Mark DeYmaz and Bob Whitesel provide a compelling call for churches everywhere to challenge the status quo regardless of where they find themselves.
By providing a balance of scriptural, social, and practical considerations, *re:MIX*
provides a path forward for any community to realize the profound beauty of
the church in living color."
—Constance Cherry, Professor of Christian Worship and Pastoral Ministry, Indiana Wesleyan University, Marion, IN

Other Books by the Authors

Mark DeYmaz

Building a Healthy Multi-Ethnic Church

Leading a Healthy Multi-Ethnic Church

Should Pastors Accept or Reject the Homogeneous Unit Principle?

The Multi-Ethnic Christian Life Primer

Bob Whitesel

Organix: Signs of Leadership in a Changing Church

Inside the Organic Church: Learning from 12 Emerging Congregations

*Growth by Accident, Death by Planning: How Not to
Kill a Growing Congregation*

*Staying Power! Why People Leave the Church Over Change and
What You Can Do About It*

*A House Divided: Bridging the Generation Gaps in
Your Church* (with Kent R. Hunter)

Foundations of Church Administration (General Editor and Contributor)

Additional books from other publishers are available from your
favorite bookseller.

re:MIX

Transitioning Your Church to Living Color

Mark DeYmaz & Bob Whitesel

Abingdon Press™

Nashville

RE:MIX
TRANSITIONING YOUR CHURCH TO LIVING COLOR

Copyright © 2016 by Mark DeYmaz and Bob Whitesel

This book is printed on acid-free paper.

Library of Congress Cataloging-in-Publication Data

Names: DeYmaz, Mark, 1961- author.
Title: re:MIX : transitioning your church to living color / Mark DeYmaz, Bob Whitesel.
Description: First [edition] | Nashville, Tennessee : Abingdon Press, 2016. | Includes bibliographical references.
Identifiers: LCCN 2015047961 (print) | LCCN 2016000407 (ebook) | ISBN 9781630886929 (binding: pbk.) | ISBN 9781630886936 (e-book)
Subjects: LCSH: Race relations--Religious aspects--Christianity. | Social classes. | Church.
Classification: LCC BT734.2 .D49 2016 (print) | LCC BT734.2 (ebook) | DDC 259.089--dc23
LC record available at http://lccn.loc.gov/2015047961

Scripture quotations unless noted otherwise are from the Common English Bible. Copyright © 2011 by the Common English Bible. All rights reserved. Used by permission. www.CommonEnglishBible.com.

Scripture quotations marked (NIV) are taken from the Holy Bible, New International Version®, NIV®. Copyright © 1973, 1978, 1984, 2011 by Biblica, Inc.™ Used by permission of Zondervan. All rights reserved worldwide. www.zondervan.com. The "NIV" and "New International Version" are trademarks registered in the United States Patent and Trademark Office by Biblica, Inc.™

Scripture quotations marked (The Message) are from THE MESSAGE. Copyright © by Eugene H. Peterson 1993, 1994, 1995, 1996, 2000, 2001, 2002. Used by permission of NavPress Publishing Group.

Scripture quotations marked NRSV are from the New Revised Standard Version of the Bible, copyright 1989, Division of Christian Education of the National Council of the Churches of Christ in the United States of America. Used by permission. All rights reserved.

The list on page 98 (note 27) about the categories of Acts 2 is excerpted from *Organix: Signs of Leadership in a Changing Church* by Bob Whitesel, Copyright © 2012 by Abingdon Press. Used by permission. All rights reserved.

16 17 18 19 20 21 22 23 24 25—10 9 8 7 6 5 4 3 2 1
MANUFACTURED IN THE UNITED STATES OF AMERICA

Mark DeYmaz

To my mother, Dorothy Mae Owen DeYmaz, whose prayers for me so long ago were answered.

Bob Whitesel

To my colorful students, clients, and colleagues who for over twenty-five years have opened my eyes to the processes of spiritual and physical reconciliation. And to my college sweetheart and wife, Rebecca.

About the Cover

The single silhouette represents the coming together of nations, tribes, peoples, and tongues, as one new person, household, and holy temple of God—a church of living color—made possible through the death of Christ on the cross (Eph 2:14-22; Rev 7:9). The separate lines of color declare that in coming together, cultures do not lose their distinctiveness; rather, each contributes something unique and beautiful to the whole, "God's purpose is now to show the rulers and powers in the heavens the many different varieties of his wisdom throughout the church" (Eph 3:10).

Contents

Preface: How to Use This Book

We Live in a Time of Unprecedented Integration and Socialization

The rise of social media together with global population shifts has made the world a much smaller place. Today, men and women of diverse ethnic and economic backgrounds live closer to one another than ever before; not only in the United States but in many places around the world. We share the same neighborhoods, shop in the same stores, and work for the same companies. Our children go to the same schools, play on the same teams, and listen to the same music. At the end of the day, we share similar dreams.

There Are Personal, Corporate, and Systemic Challenges to Overcome

Where cultures collide, they tend to clash, giving rise to varying degrees of tension, animosity, and polarization. Some would argue the closer and more frequent our connections, the greater the divides between us. Such obstacles, however, provide local churches today with an unprecedented opportunity to offer a credible and compelling witness of God's love for all people.

But There Is Hope: Local Churches of Living Color

Churches of living color—healthy multiethnic and economically diverse congregations of faith—are uniquely positioned to promote peace, advance justice, and find favor in the eyes of an increasingly diverse and cynical society; more so today, in fact, than homogeneous churches that for too many years have been the objective of church planting, growth, and development. For in a society that values diversity, that which lacks it will be increasingly looked upon with suspicion, distrust, and fear.

re:MIX Your Church for the Sake of the Gospel

This book was published to help you reposition your church for long-term impact in a rapidly changing society; to reach ethnically and economically diverse people in your community; to help you build confidence, trust, and faith across distinctions and divides; and to help you advance a credible witness of God's love for all people on earth as it is in heaven. Indeed, believers from all ethnic and economic backgrounds share the same faith, hope, and love. Is it not long past time for us to share the same church, for the sake of our witness, to fulfill the Great Commission?

About This Book

This short but significant read provides food for thought, practical advice, and stories of transition as told by pastors who have led their churches through transition, from mono- to multiethnic. The authors consider reconciliation, mission, integration, and transformation as both the substance and success of the effort. They share transferrable tips to help you articulate the vision in a clear and concise way for others.

The Title Is Instructive

re:MIX is structured around the title letters to help you quickly recall and articulate for others basic building blocks that are necessary to transition a church to living color. If you are wondering where to start, see chapter 1 on creating a *Reconciling* community of faith. If you are considering the purpose of a multiethnic church, see chapter 2 on creating a *Missional* community of faith. If you are looking for ways to promote a spirit of inclusion in your church, see chapter 3 on creating an *Inclusive* community of faith. And, if you are looking ahead to where this all should lead, see chapter 4 on creating a *Transformative* community of faith.

How to Use This Book

Study the book yourself or together with your staff, lay leaders, and decision makers, or employ it as a curriculum for small groups in your church. One way or another, don't let it merely collect dust on your bookshelf. Beyond mere study, the book has also been designed as a reference guide to help you quickly find insight and direction in seeking to implement, not just contemplate, the transition of your church to living color.

Introduction

What?!
Why . . . How . . . When?
Really?!
Us? This? Now?
In our church?!
These are the questions you have heard already, or soon will face, at the suggestion of change in your church. Of course, this is not just any change you are undertaking to lead and pursue. It is *this* change. Demographic shift. Systemic transformation. A fundamental re:MIX of the status quo.

This change will require faith, courage, and sacrifice on the part of everyone involved, especially those who currently comprise the majority culture of your church, for whom most to date has been informed and purposed. It is change that will lead to some not liking it, to some leaving because of it, to some loving it, to others being drawn to it, and more importantly to spiritually at-risk people finding Christ and joining the church because of it.

It is, at once, the following:

- change the Lord requires of us, the local church, for his own glory;
- change that is biblical and expected in the New Testament;
- change that is right, gracious, and just;
- change through which you will reposition the church for long-term community engagement and impact;
- change that is the hope of the gospel in an increasingly diverse society.

Prepare yourself for a great adventure: you're about to embark on the re:MIX journey!

1

Of course, leading others through *this* change will not be easy. It will often be exhausting: emotionally, mentally, and experientially. At points you will be misunderstood, your motives misrepresented, and your actions misinterpreted. You know this is true: if not personally, yet, as you consider the road ahead. Still, you're compelled to take the first step. Why? Because you've been called to do so, seemingly prepared to do so and for this moment. Indeed, you're certain the hand of God has led you here and his voice is urging you on. You are determined, then, to inaugurate *this* change in this church, for the sake of this church and its future; for the sake of the gospel.

That's why you hold this book in your hand. That's why you've accepted the mission: to transition your church to living color.

Do these words resonate in your spirit? Can you feel it: an inner sense of peace, fulfillment, and joy as you consider the future, the possibilities? Even as you face the unknown, be assured you are not alone: God is with you. We want to be as well. That's why we wrote this book; that's what it's all about. You can do it: we can help!

A Practical Guide to Homogeneous Church Transition

re:MIX—Transitioning Your Church to Living Color is a practical guide to help you transition an otherwise homogeneous church into a healthy multiethnic and economically diverse congregation of faith for the sake of the gospel.[1] Whether your church is currently growing, plateaued, or in decline, this book can help you reposition it for future growth and vitality. In so doing, you will expand your church's impact in the community.

Before diving into the basics, sharing helpful tips, and providing insight and encouragement from other pastors who have successfully transitioned their churches to living color, as we'll do in coming chapters, let's first take a moment to consider some of what you can expect on the re:MIX journey.

Encountering Others

Confusion

The first reaction you are likely to face is confusion. Whether this confusion is expressed from within your own family or by your closest friends, by church members, lay leadership, paid staff, or denominational and network leaders, expect that some people will not understand your intentions, at first . . . at all . . . if ever. This will be discouraging—to realize they don't get it, that they're not sure about it, or about what this means for your career long-term. Such interaction will test your resolve; and it's important that it's tested. God will use these conversations to help confirm and clarify your calling.

Concern

Such clarity will be useful in navigating the broader pushback coming your way. People will offer a number of reasons for why any attempt to re:MIX the church is not wise and unwarranted. They'll cite history, tradition, context, and timing. They'll tell you why they love the church as it is, suggest that many others do too, and warn you not to rock the boat. Both in receiving and responding to their concerns, you will learn how to better articulate the vision and proactively address similar questions others will have as well. God will use this interaction to build your competence and confidence ahead of the actual transition.

Criticism

Criticism often emerges not from disagreement but from lack of good discussion. Effective communication requires time and dialogue.[2] Patiently helping people overcome their confusion and actively listening to their concerns on the front end will help mitigate criticism. In spite of your best efforts, however, you can't please everyone. Expect some to leave the church for another, and to denigrate you in the process. But remember, God's got this (John 14:1). Do not let disparaging comments bring you down or pull you off mission. Forgive, forget, and move on.

Commendation

In the midst of confusion, concern, and criticism expressed by some, many others will commend your mind, heart, will, and motives. From these you will draw encouragement and strength; thank God for them! As much as you need to listen to the uncertain responses of others, you will want and need even more to pour into people ready, willing, and able to advance the vision alongside you through relationships or service. Commendation will come not only from those within the church but also from believers throughout the city, and even the community itself—a secular community that readily respects any attempt to bring diverse people together across race, class, and cultural divides. All such validation will add fuel to your fire, a fire that will soon burn even brighter in the next zone of your re:MIX experience.

Experiencing God

Mission

Understanding that pursuit of a healthy multiethnic church is biblical, that other pastors have successfully led the transition of homogeneous congregations, and that a number of promising practices are already in place as you will discover throughout this book, you should feel a sense of excitement as you begin to advance the mission. Your faith, like a muscle, will be exercised and grow. As it does, so will the faith of others. Together, you have accepted a significant calling. The writer of Hebrews said, "Without faith it is impossible to please God" (Heb 11:6 NRSV). And make no mistake: your faith and this mission is pleasing to God.

Mystery

Pastors of multiethnic churches often feel as though they're living in the pages of the New Testament, walking in the footsteps of the Apostle Paul, and witnessing the mystery of Gentile inclusion play out through the growth and development of unity and diversity in their churches. Paul defines this ancient mystery in his letters to the churches in Rome (Rom 16:25-26), Colossians (Col 1:24-27), and Ephesus (Eph 3:2-6). The mystery of Gentile inclusion is essentially this: that the gospel, the local church, and the kingdom of God are not just for one kind of people, but for all kinds of people (Eph 3:6). The church is to reflect and testify to this through its unity and diversity, on earth as it will one day be in heaven (Eph 2:11–4:6).

Miracles

According to Christ himself, we are never as close to him as we are when we are seeking to be peacemakers (Matt 5:9)—when we are helping individuals make peace with God and collectively with one another "beyond the distinctions of this world that so often and otherwise divide."[3] As you seek to advance peace in and through your church, expect to see God work in ways that can only be attributed to him: in bringing wonderfully diverse people and potential leaders to the church; in answering incredibly specific prayers; in opening for you new doors and possibilities to represent Christ and the church in the community.

Marvel

In and through all such personal encounters with God, you will at times sit back and marvel at what God is doing, what he has done, and how he is using you beyond what you might otherwise have ever sought or imagined. In the midst of Sunday services, as diverse people worship as one, people will shed tears, and you will too. In fact, they will tell you they couldn't stop crying during the service and don't know why; that they sense God in this place, in ways they've never before in a church; that this is how they always thought the church should be and look. In such moments, you will marvel, stand in awe, and give him praise. You can't take the credit. To God be the glory; great things he has done.

About the Book

To be clear, the *re:* in re:MIX stands for *reconciliation*. It is the foundation and necessary first order of business for a church of living color to tackle. And that's what we'll discuss in chapter 1. In chapters 2-4, then, we'll explain the why and how of creating a healthy multiethnic community of missional, inclusive, and transformative faith. In chapter 5, the conclusion, we'll help you think through ways to build momentum for long-term sustainability and advance of the gospel. Throughout it all, we've included the testimony and additional insights of pastors from varying denominations and locations throughout the country, all to encourage and help inform your efforts.

So . . .

Demographic shift. Systemic transformation. A fundamental re:MIX of the status quo. This is what your church needs, and now is the moment to advance. In so doing, you will experience hardship at times, yes: but even more, the deep joy, satisfaction, and reward that come from knowing you have heard the voice of God, taken steps of faith, stayed the course, and led your church to become a vibrant example for others of God's love for all people on earth as it is in heaven. It all begins with creating a reconciling community of faith. So turn the page, and let's get started.

re: Create a *Reconciling* Community of Faith

All of these new things are from God, who reconciled us to himself through Christ and who gave us the ministry of reconciliation.

—2 Corinthians 5:18

As the youth pastor at Mosaic Church in Little Rock, in 2007, Amos Gray put together a historic evening to mark the fiftieth anniversary of the integration of Little Rock Central High School (1957). Little Rock Central is a registered National Historic Site in recognition of the role it played in desegregating public schools following the US Supreme Court's ruling in *Brown v. Board of Education* (1954).

On the platform that night was Amos's aunt, Elsie. Elsie was one of three African Americans to integrate Hall High School (Little Rock) in 1959. Also on the platform was a white female classmate of Elsie's at Hall High, a woman we'll call Mary. To offer a lesson in civil rights history, Elsie and Mary spoke that night of race relations then and now, of progress that's been made, and of what remains to be done.

Although the two women did not know one another personally in high school, Mary had never forgotten that Elsie was one of her classmates. That evening, she recalled witnessing some of the harsh treatment that Elsie had endured. As the only African American in Hall High's class of 1962, Elsie shared that fellow students had treated her unfairly and often directed hatred toward her. She carried this hurt and a measure of bitterness toward her classmates through the years. Not once did she attend a class reunion.

The significance of Elsie and Mary being involved with Amos that evening was that they had attended Hall High together at the height of the civil rights movement, yet had otherwise not spoken to each other in fifty years. With this in mind, Amos had brought these women together half a century later to encourage and model the power of lament, forgiveness, and reconciliation before the diverse students and adults of Mosaic.

Reflecting on their historic days in high school, Elsie and Mary not only enlightened those in attendance that night but also listened to each other's hearts. Throughout their lives painful memories had affected them deeply. By the end of the evening, however, both women had come to see themselves as sisters in Christ. Amos had the historic and heartwarming opportunity to lead the women in a prayer of forgiveness and reconciliation. Afterward, Elsie embraced Mary as Mary expressed sorrow over not doing anything at the time to help end the harsh treatment Elsie had endured. Throughout the sanctuary, tears were shed.

Elsie and Mary went on to spend even more time with each other in the years following the event. Together they attended Hall High's fiftieth reunion of the class of 1962 in 2012.[1]

Racism Is Ultimately a Spiritual Problem

This story illustrates the unique platform a multiethnic church has to promote and encourage authentic reconciliation in a diverse and often polarized (along the lines of race and class) society. Indeed, a church of living color can become an anchor of hope within its community. In sowing seeds of reconciliation, its good work will bring glory to God (Matt 5:16). Sadly, though, the far more common segregation of local churches today has the world looking elsewhere for advice when it comes to matters of race, class, and culture.

For example, the day after a jury in Sanford, Florida, found George Zimmerman not guilty in the shooting death of Trayvon Martin, *USA Today*'s front-page headline (July 15, 2013) asked, "After Zimmerman verdict, can nation heal racial rift?" Similarly, we might ask: Given the historic alienation between whites and blacks, as well as between whites and Native Americans, in the United States; the complex realities of undocumented immigrants among us; and human nature itself, is racial reconciliation even possible?

Many believe that our society is without hope in this regard. We, however, think differently.

Yes, it is incumbent upon local churches and, therefore, on the pastors who lead them to pursue and practice the ministry of reconciliation, something to which we, the body of Christ, have been called. That we should do so is expected by Christ himself, as explained by the Apostle Paul in 2 Corinthians 5:16-21.

To be clear, the ministry of reconciliation the Apostle Paul has in mind is not only to be pursued at a personal level (in seeing individuals reconciled to God through faith in Jesus Christ); it is to be pursued at a corporate one as well (in seeing men and women of varying backgrounds reconciled to one another through the blood of Christ, in and through the local church, as explained by Paul in Ephesians 2:11-22).

According to the latest research, churches today are ten times more segregated than the neighborhoods in which they exist, and twenty times more segregated than nearby public schools.[2] To our collective shame, eleven o'clock on Sunday morning remains the most segregated hour of the week. Thus, the hope and benefit of reconciliation remains elusive; for it cannot be fully realized in our society until we first deal with systemic segregation in the local church. This we can do; this dream you can realize, by transitioning your church to living color.

Of course, measurable progress will require more than wishful thinking. Since "racism is ultimately a spiritual problem, it will require a spiritual solution."[3] Therefore, the primary purpose, task, and responsibility of the local church is to promote reconciliation between individuals and God, as well as between individuals themselves, for the sake of the gospel. This is what the Apostle Paul has in mind in reiterating to the churches of Galatia what Christ told a legal expert in Luke 10:23-27. After explaining that in Christ (that is, for Christians) what matters to God is not one's vain attempt to keep the Law but rather one's faith working through love (for God and neighbor), Paul writes: "All the Law has been fulfilled in a single statement: Love your neighbor as yourself" (Gal 5:14).

With such things in mind, encouraging racial reconciliation in society without first establishing it in the church will likely generate more rhetoric than results. To advance a credible witness, we must re:MIX the church.

To date, however, the inability, unwillingness, or lack of intentionality on the part of local church pastors in seeking to bring diverse people together as one in the church has rendered us, collectively, impotent in the eyes of society on matters of race, class, and injustice. In other words, people instinctively look elsewhere for answers; they do not look to the local church.

For example, when tensions arose after a grand jury failed to indict Officer Darren Wilson in the shooting death of Michael Brown in Ferguson, Missouri, the national media turned to lawyers, government and law enforcement officials, actors and actresses, educators, journalists, psychologists, sociologists, and the like, for understanding and commentary. By and large, however, pastors (and particularly evangelical pastors) were not even invited in to the discussion; most certainly, none that were white. Later, the same was true when tensions arose in the aftermath of the choking death of Eric Garner in Staten Island, New York, following an Ohio grand jury's failure to indict Officer Timothy Loehmann in the shooting death of twelve-year-old Tamir Rice in Cleveland, and the list goes on.

Such isolation from public dialogue should concern us: for the church to be sidelined in the discussion of what is and should be just in our society negatively affects our ability to proclaim a just and loving (of all people) God and to be genuinely heard by the ones he came to save. According to Micah 6:8, doing justice is what the Lord requires of us. And here's the kicker: we have the answer—the Prince of Peace, Christ our Lord, who by his own blood abolished the enmity (historical animosity, deep-seated hatred) between us—Jews and Gentiles, poor and rich, male and female (Gal 3:28). The problem, though, is no one is listening: for an increasingly diverse population does not and will not accept mere platitudes apart from practice. It does not embrace theological rhetoric that is undermined by the very real division of churches along ethnic and economic lines.

Simply put, when it comes to addressing such things, the American church lacks credibility. But we should not at all blame the media. Collective irrelevance is a reflection of us: our personal preferences, philosophical priorities, and self-serving church-growth strategies that continue to inform our praxis. Perhaps this quote from an article in the *Christian Post* says it best:

> For far too long we have turned a blind eye to the lack of diversity within our congregations; proudly championed homogeneity in church planting;

celebrated numeric growth and attendance more than community revitalization and transformation; encouraged the purchase of land and building
new buildings instead of repurposing abandoned space in the community
as a physical manifestation of the power and message of redemption; re-
fused to empower minority leadership or to share authoritative responsibility in otherwise all-white churches; and the list goes on.[4]

For these and other reasons, we must not fail in this moment to recognize that racial divides in the United States are not drawing people to
Christ, to the church, and to one another, but driving them further away
from his love, and ours. The time is now to transition your church to living color; that is, for otherwise systemically segregated and homogeneous
congregations to become more a reflection of their increasingly diverse
communities than they are a reflection of one demographic group or another. In healthy multiethnic churches, men and women of varying backgrounds—reconciled to God and to one another through Jesus Christ—
will authenticate the gospel. Together, they will proclaim with power, in
more than words, its message of faith, hope, and love in a world desperate
for peace.

As stated already, we do believe that achieving the dream of a racially
integrated and reconciled society is possible; but only if and when churches
that model it saturate the landscape. Yes, churches of living color will inspire its pursuit, and more importantly become a most powerful, credible,
and attractive witness for Christ. To make this our goal is not at all to suc-
cumb or champion political correctness. Rather, it is to elevate biblical
correctness—the ministry of individual *and* collective reconciliation—to
front and center in our churches, where the latter of which should have
been equally declared and pursued all along.

St. Paul's United Methodist Church • Asheville, North Carolina

From the Desk of Pastor In-Yong Lee

In 2013, in an effort to revitalize my congregation, I began
to champion a multiethnic vision at St. Paul's UMC. Not long
after, on our sign out front, the church asked the community

the same question it was asking itself: "If the kingdom of God is not segregated, why on earth is the church?" Overnight, though, vandals repositioned the sign's words to read: "The kingdom of racists." So how did our church respond?

First, by covering the words with a red sheet to convey a message of lament. Then, the next day, by posting a prayer on the sign: "Lord, help us to become a church that truly reflects heaven." In so doing, we responded in humility. "Thank you for interacting with us," we said. "You see Christians as racists. Forgive us. We are trying to change. Come try with us."

Understanding Reconciliation

To transition your church to living color, you will need to reconsider your understanding of reconciliation. To do so, let's take a moment to think biblically, historically, and contextually.

Think Biblically

For far too long the American church has compartmentalized the notions of lament, repentance, reconciliation, and justice, as alluded to in our introduction. In other words, religious leaders typically discuss, encourage, promote, or fail to deal with one or more of these concepts at any given time. But here's the reality: lament, repentance, reconciliation, and justice are not concepts peripheral to the gospel; they are intrinsic to it. Once we understand this, pursuit of reconciliation in and through the local church will not be seen as optional, but as it should be—biblical.

The word *reconciliation* means "to change, exchange, as coins for others of equivalent value . . . return to favor with . . . [or] to receive one into favor."[5] Scripture itself places reconciliation at the very heart and purpose of Christ's ministry and mission. For example, the Apostle Paul writes, "We were reconciled to God through the death of his Son while we were still enemies" (Rom 5:10). Notice this verse, though written to a church, speaks primarily of our individual reconciliation to God through faith in Jesus Christ. Likewise, Paul speaks to us as individuals in Ephesians 1:3-11, where he highlights the benefits of our redemption (reconciliation to God) through his blood.

But reconciliation is not just something we are to pursue or experience individually. The fact is, we are expected to advance reconciliation collectively as well. So Paul writes to the church at Corinth,

> All of these new things are from God, who reconciled us to himself through Christ and who gave us the ministry of reconciliation. In other words, God was reconciling the world to himself through Christ, by not counting people's sins against them. He has trusted us with this message of reconciliation. So we are ambassadors who represent Christ. God is negotiating with you through us. We beg you as Christ's representatives, "Be reconciled to God!" (2 Cor 5:18-20)

Not surprisingly, Jesus anticipated that individuals, having been reconciled to God, would be reconciled to one another in and through the local church. Diverse believers who will themselves to walk, work, and worship God together as one in the church declare an uncommon testimony before the world that authenticates the gospel. On the night before he died, Jesus prayed that his followers would "be one, Father, just as you are in me and I am in you. I pray that they also will be in us, so that the world will believe that you sent me. . . . So that they will be made perfectly one. Then the world will know that you sent me and that you have loved them just as you loved me" (John 17:21, 23).

Not only as individuals, then, but also collectively through the local church, we are to be ambassadors of God advancing the ministry of reconciliation. God has given this ministry to us and entrusted the church with it. Through our authentic witness of faith, hope, and love (1 Cor 13:13), we "negotiate" with a wide variety of people on God's behalf beyond the distinctions of this world that so often divide. A church of living color represents Christ well, then, by providing a credible and inspiring witness of God's love for all people, attracting diverse others to come be reconciled to God and to one another.

Think Historically

Even in the first century, reconciliation was desperately needed where race, class, and gender were concerned. So Paul instructed the churches of Galatia, "You are all God's children through faith in Christ Jesus. All of you who were baptized into Christ have clothed yourselves with Christ. There is neither Jew nor Greek; there is neither slave nor free; nor is there male and female, for you all are one in Christ Jesus" (Gal 3:26-28).

Paul writes similarly to the church at Colossae (Col 3:11). James, too, challenged his readers to cease from honoring those with wealth at the expense of the poor (Jas 2:1-9).

Why then do churches so often cater to one demographic group at the expense of another? What makes us want to establish churches filled with people who look just like us? Sure, it's easier; but nowhere in the Bible do we get a pass on degree of difficulty. Indeed, we have been called to establish churches that reflect the will of God, not our own.

As much as anything, the division of local churches along ethnic and economic lines has been perpetuated by the misapplication of what is known as the Homogeneous Unit Principle (HUP). According to the principle's progenitor and recognized father of the modern church growth movement, Donald A. McGavran, the HUP recognized that "[people] like to become Christians without crossing racial, linguistic or class barriers."[6] In the early 1970s, however, this was reinterpreted to suggest that churches grow fastest when they're homogeneous. And this is right; they do. But as Chuck Swindoll has said, "Jesus never suggested that crowds were the goal. He never addresses getting your church to grow. Never. So why is that the emphasis today?"[7]

Even today, this misunderstanding of the HUP is how pastors are typically instructed to plant, grow, and develop a church. While we do not at all mean to question motives, it otherwise fuels unintentionally a spirit of competition not cooperation, independence not interdependence, self-importance not self-sacrifice, and success within the American church largely measured by Sunday morning attendance.

However, the HUP was never intended as a strategy for building big churches quickly filled with people who are generally alike, but for reaching diverse people who do not yet know Christ as we do—particularly people outside the United States and overseas. According to Donald McGavran, the HUP is "primarily a missionary and an evangelistic principle."[8] McGavran also warned that with any misunderstanding or misapplication of the HUP, "there is a danger that congregations . . . become exclusive, arrogant, and racist. That danger must be resolutely combated."[9]

In other words, McGavran's understanding of the HUP—a principle he, himself, mined and articulated—was never meant to separate us along

14

the lines of race and class. Indeed he understood and expected, as did the Apostle Paul, that a local church should reflect God's wonderfully diverse kingdom on earth, wherever possible, and get beyond race and class distinctions in this world that so typically keep us apart.

The church has a checkered past in terms of advancing a ministry of reconciliation. But the Spirit's power to transform our hearts, minds, and churches must not be held captive to past failings. The supernatural power that reconciles us first to God and then to one another, wonderfully on display in churches of living color, is desperately needed in a world today filled with ethnic and economic tensions.

Think Contextually

Today, there's a growing cultural mix of people, personalities, and past experiences surrounding established churches. Neighborhoods, communities, cities, and towns are changing. And with their own growth and sustainability in mind, they no longer describe themselves as "culturally distinct"; rather, they are seeking to become even more diverse and to celebrate diversity.

These demographic and attitudinal shifts afford us the opportunity to transition existing churches away from homogeneity to better reflect the kingdom of God on earth as it is in heaven and, in the process, position our churches for future growth and vitality. Toward that end, we must seize the day. Indeed, for the sake of the gospel, we must advance the ministry of reconciliation in order to build cross-cultural relationships and competence with people of varying language, culture, and custom. Today, this means people living not only across an ocean but also across the street from us. Congregations who are unwilling to re:MIX can expect a steady decline in membership and relevance over time.

Along with the growing ethnic and economic diversity of people living in and around our churches, people are living longer as well. We should consider how to expand generational diversity, too, in transitioning the church to living color. Here's an overview of just some of the designations used today:

- **Ethnic designations** include: Anglo, non-Hispanic white, Hispanic, Latin American, Hispanic American, African American, Asian American, and Native American.[10]

- **Socioeconomic designations** include: Upper Socioeconomic Level, Upper Middle Socioeconomic Level, Lower Middle Socioeconomic Level, Working Socioeconomic Level, and Lower Socioeconomic Level.[11]

- **Generational designations** (reflecting people alive today) include: Millennials (though their birth years range by a few decades among social scientists, for this book we will describe them as born 2003 or later), Generation Y (1984–2002), Generation X (1965–1983), Baby Boomers (1946–1964), the Greatest (or Silent) Generation (prior to 1945).[12]

With such things in mind, here are some key facts concerning the current context:

- "More than half of children born today belong to racial and ethnic groups traditionally thought of as minorities," as are one in two children under the age of five. By 2018, one in two young people under the age of eighteen will be nonwhite as well.[13]

- "In 2004, nearly 60 percent of public school children were white. By 2014, the percentage had fallen to 49.7 percent, marking the first time in U.S. history that a majority of students were from minority groups. By 2022 the percentage of white students is projected to fall to 45 percent."[14]

- "Millennials [born 2003 or later] are the most racially diverse generation in American history. Some 43% of Millennial adults are non-white, the highest share of any generation."[15]

- By 2060, 57 percent of Americans will be people of color (black, Hispanic, and other).[16]

- Cultural discrimination remains high but is seen more often by people of color. Thirty-five percent of African Americans said they have "personally experienced discrimination or been treated unfairly because of their race or ethnicity over the past year . . . compared with 20% of Hispanics and 10% of whites."[17]

- Between 2000 and 2010 "the percentage of multi[ethnic] congregations (using the 20 percent or more minority criteria [pertaining to attending members]) had nearly doubled . . . to 13.7 percent. . . . In 2010, 12.5 percent of all Protestant Christian churches and 27.1 percent of other Christian churches (Catholic/Orthodox) were multi[ethnic]. Multi[ethnic] Mainline Protestant churches accounted for 7.4 percent of their total, while 14.4 percent of Evangelical Protestant congregations were multi[ethnic]."[18]

- Churches that do become multiethnic are some of the best places to break down cultural barriers.[19]

Dayspring Church (Church of God, Anderson, Indiana) • Cincinnati, Ohio

There Is No Plan B

Pastor Tim Kufeldt

Dayspring Church is situated on the I-275 corridor in northern Cincinnati. Dayspring was a predominantly homogeneous white congregation that, during the course of her seventy-six-year history, relocated twice, each time moving farther away from the heart of the city.

Fourteen years ago, when I came to Dayspring, our fellowship included only a few people of color. Though the surrounding county contained 47 percent nonwhites, only 2 percent of our congregation was nonwhite. In fact, of the 275 family units who were on our rosters, only five were comprised of people of color, whether Black, Asian, Latino, or non-European internationals.

Thankfully, Dayspring Church is now fully integrated with 38 percent nonwhites in our English-speaking service. In addition, we have two international fellowships: a Latino ministry and a small group of Southwestern Pacific Islanders. Today our fellowship includes members who are Caucasian, African American, and many others who have come from the far reaches of the globe: Antigua, South Africa, Nigeria, Kenya, Cameroon, South and Central Americas, Philippines, Ghana, India, Papua New Guinea, Chile, and Costa Rica. It is true that our demographics now reflect a near mirror of the surrounding community.

17

Several factors helped us make this journey into ethnic diversity: the Great Commission required it and our diverse community demanded it. If we are going to be faithful to reach our own Jerusalem, we have no other choice but to purposely extend ourselves to all people, whatever their ethnicity, and invite them into our fellowship.

So, how did we re:MIX?

- We prayed for our diverse community. We went house-to-house, collecting prayer concerns and praying over anyone who allowed us to. This sparked a spiritual connection with our neighbors.

- We began to proclaim our future reality in present language and identity. Even before we were diverse we adopted the motto: Dayspring . . . Where the Nations Worship.

- We displayed flags of the nations represented in our church both inside and outside our worship center.

- We made sure to represent diversity in every image, promotional material, and media presentation.

- We engaged ethnically diverse leaders in every worship experience. Our worship musical style purposefully reflected the styles, hearts, and languages of those in our surrounding communities.

- We have been willing to pay the price. With change there will always be people who don't like it and who will stand in the way. As the leader, I gave people no other option: this is God's will, God's timing, and God's purpose for us. We lost some good people along the way, those not quite ready for change. It was costly and painful, but we've stayed the course.

In John 4, the Bible tells us that Jesus had to go through Samaria. The text is written in such a way to suggest that there was a divine appointment waiting for him; he had to follow the will of his Father. In so doing, he was constrained to leave behind the more familiar path and to travel through an area with which he was not accustomed.

Likewise, God is compelling us to leave our comfort zones, the ways of segregation, behind us in order to experience the church on earth as Christ intended. Indeed, God has one agenda: reconciliation. We are to be reconciled to God and reconciled to one another across race and class distinctions to proclaim a credible gospel.

Let me confess to you, I am passionate about diversity! Indeed, I am thoroughly convinced that God calls the church to be on earth as it is in heaven (Rev 7:9). I believe there is no other option. I am sold out for the cause! There is no Plan B.

At Dayspring, then, reconciliation is our battle cry. I pray it will become yours as well.

re:MIX for Reconciliation

We must do more than think about reconciliation to transition a church to living color. As pastors, we must be intentional in its pursuit. This will require you to make some adjustments in your personal approach to ministry and some structural adjustments in your church as well. Change is never easy, but to establish a ministry of reconciliation you'll need to expand your pastoral sphere of influence and reposition the church for future credibility in an increasingly diverse community.

Personal Adjustments

Get Outside of Your Bubble

A very prominent, internationally recognized white pastor was recently asked if he knew of Dr. John M. Perkins, one of the leading Christ-centered voices to come out of the American civil rights movement and founder of the Christian Community Development Association. The pastor said, "Nope, never heard of him." Given the equally recognized accomplishments of Dr. Perkins, who is African American, it was a stark reminder of how siloed one can become within his or her own sphere of influence. To get outside of your bubble:

- **Share a meal.** Invite someone of a different ethnic or economic background to share a meal with you, to your home for a family function, or to attend an event highlighting his or her culture.

- **Spend an hour at Walmart.** Write down your perception of the racial diversity, or lack thereof, in close proximity to your church. Then go spend an hour sitting just inside the nearest Walmart to see if the diversity you witness there matches your perception.

- **Walk the halls of your church.** Walk into the nursery, children's ministry classrooms, or halls in your church. Observe the dolls in the cribs or other toys depicting people. Look at the pictures of Jesus on the walls. Do such things communicate to diverse others a love for all people or just one kind of person? Do they communicate that everyone is welcome, or only certain ones?

- **Visit local schools.** The local school system(s) from which your congregants are drawn is one of the easiest and most reliable sources of demographic insight. You will often find that the school system is comprised of students with dozens of birth languages. Many school systems can provide you with demographic forecasts too. This will help you grasp the current and emerging cultures in your sphere of influence.

- **Follow the bread crumbs.** At any given time, various people groups within a city are putting on one event or another. The city itself is likely hosting events to bring diverse people together. Research these events and contact organizers to see how you and your church can volunteer, sponsor, or rent a booth. By showing an interest in diverse people of the city and their passions, you will soon develop new friends and a reputation of inclusion. In time you will be invited to other such events to help plan them, to sit on city boards or planning commissions, and the like, gaining broader understanding and influence. Follow the relational bread crumbs and a whole new world of diverse relationships and unique possibilities will open up for you.

Invest in Cross-Cultural Friendships

Fundamentally, reconciliation cannot be addressed at a structural level until it has been embraced at a personal level, within your own heart. Only then will you be motivated and excited to pursue this biblical calling with others of a different ethnic or economic background. With this in mind, consider the following questions:

1. With whom are you now forging friendships of genuine transparency and trust?

2. To whom can you go to begin a conversation and, more important, begin to listen?

3. With which diverse friends can you mark culturally historical moments, attend expressive activities and artistic events, or celebrate family traditions?

Multicultural friendships can be easy to initiate but harder to maintain for a variety of reasons. That said, they are nothing to fear. Rather, they are something many people of varying ethnic heritage genuinely want to develop. To begin and maintain these relationships will require intentional effort on your part, namely, prayer, patience, and persistence. Among other things, you will have to do the following:

Exercise Humility and Gentleness (Eph 4:2)

Ask diverse others what you need to hear and learn from them, or what they've been reluctant to tell you about yourself or your culture.

Listen Well and Patiently (Jas 1:19)

Be quick to hear and slow to speak. Inquire not only of the individual's story, but also of his or her collective story related to culture. Resist the urge to comment in the moment; you can do so later, once you have more prayerfully processed what you've heard.

Be Open and Honest (Phil 2:2-3)

Discuss differences; admit prejudices and stereotypes; inquire as to another's feeling or sense of cross-cultural injustice and pain.

Express Lament and Extend Apology (Lev 26:40-42)

Majority-culture individuals are often reluctant to express such things when it comes to the past. By definition, though, lament is a passionate expression of grief or sorrow, and apology involves a regretful acknowledgment of an offense or failure. We should not be afraid to express such things collectively for the sake of reconciliation and healing. Where there is privilege or power, it should be acknowledged, leveraged, and shared for the greater good.

Care for One Another (1 Cor 12:14-26)

This applies not only to individuals but to entire people groups; as the scripture says, "so that there won't be division in the body [specifically, along Jew and Gentile lines at the time] and so the parts might have mutual concern for each other" (v. 25). Likewise, the Apostle Paul writes to the church at Philippi, "Instead of each person watching out for their own good, watch out for what is better for others" (Phil 2:4).

Your willingness to initiate and ultimately develop multicultural friendships and relationships is critical to your pursuit and acquisition of cross-cultural competence. You will need both to effectively re:MIX your church and lead it in the years ahead.

Read Books and Articles

Dr. John A. Kirk is the George W. Donaghey Distinguished Professor of History and department chair at the University of Arkansas at Little Rock, in Little Rock, Arkansas. He is a world-renowned expert in "the history of the civil rights movement in the United States, the South, . . . and the history of post–New Deal southern politics, society and culture."[20]

For pastors seeking to gain cross-cultural competence, Dr. Kirk recommends the following books:[21]

- David Garrow, *Bearing the Cross: Martin Luther King, Jr., and the Southern Christian Leadership Conference*

- Isabel Wilkerson, *The Warmth of Other Suns: The Epic Story of America's Great Migration*

- Carolyn DuPont, *Mississippi Praying: Southern White Evangelicals and the Civil Rights Movement, 1945–1975*

Watch Documentaries

Similarly, Dr. Kirk suggests the following films and documentaries for viewing and discussion in small groups:

- *Eyes on the Prize* (PBS)
- *Slavery by Another Name* (PBS)
- *Little Rock Central: 50 Years Later* (HBO)

Structural Adjustments

Teach the Biblical Mandate

For yourself and your congregation, it's imperative that you begin with the Bible. You must become familiar with and competent in communicating biblical expectations concerning God's heart for reconciliation, and more specifically for the nations to walk, work, and worship God together as one . . . not only in heaven someday (Rev 7:9) but right here on earth as well (Isa 56:7; Matt 21:13).

So, as you begin to re:MIX, familiarize yourself with the theology and ecclesiology of the New Testament church. For instance, do you know that Christ envisioned the multiethnic church on the night before he died, that Luke describes it in action at a place called Antioch, or that Paul prescribes it in the book of Ephesians?[22] It's important that you do! For when the time is right, as we'll discuss in another chapter, you'll need to provide sound instruction from the pulpit. And long afterward, you'll continue to answer questions from parishioners who are eager to change and skeptics, too, always pointing them to scripture.

Similar to how once you purchase a new car you begin to see it on the road everywhere, when you discover this theme of multiethnic reconciliation in God's word, you will see it everywhere you turn in the Bible, particularly in the New Testament as it concerns the church. Indeed, there's a clear and consistent thread running cover to cover that expresses God's heart for reconciliation not only of individuals to himself, but of individuals and entire people groups to one another in and through the local church for his glory.

Pastor Dana Baker of Grace Chapel in Lexington, Massachusetts, highlights God's intentions for a reconciled humanity, in part, through the following passages.[23] Become familiar with these twelve passages and teach through them at some point to establish a heart for reconciliation within the congregation. Add your own examples. There are many more such passages throughout scripture.

1. God's Expectation (Gen 1:28)

2. Babel's Folly (Gen 11:1-9)

3. Abram's Call (Gen 12:3)

4. Israel's Law (Lev 19:33)

5. Ruth's Reality (Ruth 2:10)

6. Isaiah's Reminder (Isa 2:2)

7. Samaria's Inclusion (John 4:4-10, 21, 39-42)

8. Christ's Prayer (John 17:20-23)

9. Pentecost's Restoration (Acts 2)

10. Antioch's Pattern (Acts 11:19-26; 13:1)

11. Paul's Mystery (Eph 3:2-6)

12. Heaven's Celebration (Rev 7:9)

Apply the Seven Core Commitments

According to the book *Building a Healthy Multi-Ethnic Church*, researchers and practitioners alike determined seven core commitments that are fundamental to developing vibrant churches of living color. These should be studied and applied in any attempt to re:MIX an otherwise homogeneous congregation.[24]

1. Embrace dependence.

2. Take intentional steps.

3. Empower diverse leaders.

4. Develop cross-cultural relationships.

5. Pursue cross-cultural competence.

6. Promote a spirit of inclusion.

7. Mobilize for impact.

Read The Healthy Church: Practical Ways to Strengthen a Church's Heart

1. Learn about five types of multicultural (multiethnic) churches.

2. Use the diagrams to compare and contrast the five options.

3. Determine the one that is right for you in the chapter titled "The Church as Mosaic: Exercises for Cultural Diversity."[25]

Peoples Church (Assemblies of God) • Cincinnati, Ohio

Laying Down Our Lives for the Sake of Others

Pastor Chris Beard

In 1995 God began revealing a new vision for First Christian Assembly of God in Cincinnati (now Peoples Church); a vision for a church like heaven (Rev 7:9). At the time we had no idea how a racially reconciling church could grow out of a 98 percent white commuter church, but God had a plan. It began with intentional friendships built across races with African American church leaders in our city for connection and mentoring that would provide us with insights into lives different from ours.

Four months after I became the lead pastor, race riots broke out in Cincinnati due to the shooting of Timothy Thomas, an unarmed black youth, in 2001. This same week we were interviewing our first staff pastor of color, holding the board meeting in our home due to a curfew in the city. We realized that we could not lead our church to become diverse racially if we did not have diversity in our leadership.

By 2004 we had revised our mission statement to include our desire to be a racially reconciling, generationally rich, life-giving church thriving in the heart of the city. Over time, this has dramatically impacted every aspect of church life. Every small group, every team, every event at Peoples Church has a goal to be racially and generationally rich. God gave us John 17:20-23 as an underpinning for diverse unity with the ultimate intention that "the world will believe" (v. 21).

Around that same time, we held our first Vision Experience using curriculum developed in-house with a team of laypersons and pastors. Groups of fifteen to twenty people, diverse

25

racially and generationally, met for twenty weeks, learning the differences in backgrounds and histories across the congregation. This was critical in growing understanding among the people. Consequentially, we later developed a course we called Crossonomics, a small-group experience to discuss and learn of the socioeconomic diversity among us, and what God's word has to say about that.

In 2013 we held Listening Sessions with what were, by then, our six major people groups: African American, East African, West African, Latino, Caucasian, and Asian. These were critical in order to hear from each group how better to incorporate its culture into all aspects of Peoples Church. Indeed, there are hurdles to overcome when the demographics of our church break down like this: 50 percent Caucasian, 25 percent African American, and 25 percent internationals from thirty different nations.

One critical outcome we have learned: in churches of living color, it will be a necessity to be comfortable with the uncomfortable. In other words, everyone involved has to defer at times to the preferences of others. This requires great patience and flexibility from people of all cultures. Of course, this is the life of following Christ—laying down our own lives for the sake of others (Phil 2:4).

So, from 2001 until 2015, we have grown our overall attendance numerically by about 20 percent yet have retained about 35 percent of the original group. And I won't lie: change has been difficult. Starting with a one-hundred-year-old church may have made change slightly more difficult for us, even though our church has a history of implementing new visions. Nevertheless, as you know, people choose to move to different congregations for a variety of reasons, which is always a challenge when pastoring. This is true for us.

Continually, then, we seek the face of God and God's vision for Peoples Church. Prayer is an essential part of our journey. Hearing God's voice among the clatter of diverse opinions can be a challenge. Therefore we pray for courage as we walk faithfully into the future, seeking to reflect the love of God for all people through our love for one another, in a church of living color.

Conclusion

In this chapter we've considered why, as our good friend and mentor Dr. John M. Perkins expressed long ago, *"reconciliation is the heart of the gospel."*[26] In the next chapter, we'll consider mission in a multiethnic church. Indeed, by transitioning your church to living color, you will reconcile it to the principles and practices of New Testament churches such as existed at Antioch and Ephesus. These were churches in which diverse men and women willed themselves to be one so the world would know God's love and believe. These are the churches we must again emulate today.

M: Create a *Missional* Community of Faith

I act like a Jew to the Jews, so I can recruit Jews. . . . I act like I'm outside the Law to those who are outside the Law, so I can recruit those outside the Law. . . . I have become all things to all people, so I could save some by all possible means. All the things I do are for the sake of the gospel, so I can partner with it.

—1 Corinthians 9:20-23

Elevate the Mission

On June 30, 2014, the United States Supreme Court ruled "that two for-profit corporations with sincerely held religious beliefs (Hobby Lobby and Conestoga Wood Specialties) do not have to provide a full range of contraceptives at no cost to their employees pursuant to the Affordable Care Act. . . . (T)he court held that as applied to closely held corporations the Health and Human Services regulations imposing the contraceptive mandate violate the Religious Freedom Restoration Act."[1]

As the news broke, and throughout the country, conservative Christians breathed a collective sigh of relief and "took to praising God via social media, while in the streets of an otherwise secular society there was wailing and gnashing teeth."[2]

Do you see the problem?

Deep divides that exist between the most conservative and liberal Christians, an otherwise secular society, and more broadly the role, reach, and responsibility of government—largely determined by political allegiance (whether conservative or liberal)—are today hindering local churches from advancing the gospel across race, class, and cultural lines. On the more conservative side are believers who see Christianity as fundamentally connected to the American way. According to Steven Miller, these believe that "American politics and patriotism are [at] the center of Christianity, at least as communicated in public life."[3] On the more liberal side are believers whose blogs, Facebook posts, and tweets seem more willing to advance Christian universalism than declare the uniqueness of our faith.[4]

But when did winning or losing a case at the Supreme Court or, closer to home, a war of words on Facebook or Twitter with those who do not think, vote, or believe as we do, become for us what it's all about? Indeed, is that it: the mission to which we have been called to devote and give our lives? "Make no mistake, when such things become more important than representing Christ well via social media, demonstrating the fruits of the Spirit in civil discourse, or remembering that we have been called to make disciples of all men (Republicans and Democrats, alike), Christ is not honored."[5]

Let's face it: social and political allegiances often informed by race and class contribute significantly to keeping diverse believers apart; from uniting as one to build healthy multiethnic churches; from presenting a clear and compelling gospel witness; from extending ourselves cross-culturally; from proving ourselves a credible and caring witness of God's love for all people. If we can't even walk together as one, how can we expect a diverse society to work together on any number of important social or political issues or, more significantly, to be won to Christ and to our churches?

We are not at all suggesting that Christians should refrain from social media, public discourse, or political involvement. To express one's opinions freely without fear of reprisal (thankfully) is at the heart of the American experiment. It is our right and responsibility. Nevertheless, in all such activism we should be careful not to get so caught up in the moment that we allow temporal concerns to supersede eternal mission and witness.

Christ came to seek and save the lost. He commissioned us to do the same (Matt 28:19-20).

In transitioning your church to living color you will need to keep such things in mind and, more significantly, clarify the mission at every turn. Christ (not personal or political agendas) must be lifted up if all (diverse) men and women are to be drawn to him and to your church. Indeed, Christ was sent to bring eternal life to *all* men and women (John 17:2-3); and the

Apostle Paul expects the local church to be a reflection of this mystery (Eph 3:2-6). Therefore, all men and women must be welcomed in the church and pursued, not just some; that is, not only people who look and think the same.

Multiethnic *and* Missional

In *Church 3.0*, Neil Cole describes the church at Antioch as multiethnic and missional.[6] And we agree with his assessment. In fact, while the New Testament church in Jerusalem is typically promoted as "the church to be," it's actually the church at Antioch that provides for us the best model of what a church is supposed to be—everything it can and should be.

Think about it: the church at Antioch was at once mega, missional, multisite, and multiethnic!

- It was the first church established intentionally for believing Jews and Gentiles alike (Acts 11:20).

- It was the first church to send missionaries intentionally to the world; and not just any missionaries, but the very best it had: Paul and Barnabas (Acts 13:1-3).

- It was the first church to take up a collection for the poor outside its own community (Acts 11:29).

- It was the first church in which believers were identified with Christ (Acts 11:26).

Therefore, re:MIX your church in the multiethnic and missional shadow of Antioch. Here's why.

In a healthy multiethnic church, being missional is not optional; it's natural. In other words, when people of ethnic and economic diversity are brought together in one body, a wide variety of needs and opportunities will surface. As they walk and worship God together as one, cross-cultural relationships of transparency and trust will develop and soon lead them to work together as one. Love and compassion will move such a body to missional engagement and kingdom advance. It happened at Antioch. It's happened in Little Rock. It can happen in your church too.

The reason for this is simple.

People in a healthy multiethnic church are naturally drawn to diverse people; they extend themselves to diverse people; they care for diverse people. They see themselves as having as much to learn as they have to give to others not like them in one way or another. They are friendly and welcoming; they will go where most will not. They are comfortable in a variety of settings, with a variety of people, and with a variety of challenges. They know how to pray, persevere, and remain patient. They have broader influence than their numbers otherwise suggest. They will permeate every sector of the community, not just one demographic slice of the pie.

For these reasons and more, being missional in such a church is not programmatic; it's organic.

Once you and your church understand and embrace this mindset, vision, and goal, you will begin to see the increasingly diverse people of your community as an asset, not a target. You will go to them to learn and to listen; you will invite them to come to you for the same reason. This will lead to new cross-cultural relationships, understanding, and competence. More than this, the community will begin to respect and applaud your efforts, even if it does not yet agree with your theology. All such movement is gain—a win. Follow the bread crumbs and you will soon find your way.

Pastor Dave Gibbons has suggested that in the future, a diverse society will think no different of a segregated church than we, as Christians, today think of a cult.[7] It will not respect, trust, or embrace the message of a segregated church. In other words, segregated churches will be increasingly marginalized. To avoid such a fate, lead the transition of your church today in becoming multiethnic and missional for the sake of the gospel, as our friend and fellow pastor Mark Hearn is doing in Duluth, Georgia.

First Baptist Duluth (Southern Baptist Convention) • Duluth, Georgia

Go Glocal

Pastor Mark Hearn

In March 2010 I moved from the suburbs of Indianapolis, Indiana, to become the senior pastor at First Baptist Church in Duluth. Prior to the move I researched the area and became aware of the changing landscape of the community. In part, this is what attracted me to the church. But little could prepare me for how rapidly change in the community was taking place.

In 2000, according to the US Census Bureau, Duluth was 68 percent white. By 2010, however, Duluth was only 41 percent white. The other 59 percent represented a mosaic of cultures and birth nations that revealed the enticing quality of life to be found here. I have been told that by the year 2040 every major city in America will be "majority-minority." Duluth is thirty years ahead of the curve.

Moving into a middle-class subdivision, I met neighbors next door from Korea and neighbors behind me from India. Across the street, I met a family from Zimbabwe, and at the end of the street a doctor from South Africa. My neighborhood is a microcosm of Duluth. Yet I pastored a church that remained 99 percent Anglo in the midst of this rapidly changing community. Soon, this would all change.

Mayor Nancy Harris is a member of FBC Duluth, and in the first year of my ministry here I attended her State of the City address. It soon turned into a moment of spiritual awakening. Mayor Harris quoted a statistic that day that I will never forget. She said, "There are fifty-seven languages spoken at Duluth High School." Wow! I didn't even know there were fifty-seven languages in the world! Through this revelation, I realized that *if FBC Duluth was going to make an impact on the city, it would have to become a multiethnic, multicultural congregation!*

Currently thirty-two ethnic groups are represented in our church family. In addition, we have ordained people from three different nations and more recently have added our first foreign-born ministry staff members!

Here are a few things we have learned, which I encourage you to put into practice as you seek to re:MIX your church for the glory of God:

Encourage Cross-Cultural Relationships via Small Groups

FBC Duluth has established home groups designed to foster cross-cultural relationships. We are intentional to include in these groups (known as CROSS groups) people from at least three different cultures and have at least a thirty-year age span from the oldest to the youngest group participant. Therefore, they are genuinely multigenerational, cross-cultural groups. These groups use *The Multi-Cultural Christian Life Primer* as their text.[8]

Celebrate the Diversity of Your Community

FBC Duluth loves to celebrate! And now, given our growing diversity, we have found new ways and opportunities to do so. For example, on the Sunday closest to August 15, we celebrate India's Independence Day, and on the last Sunday of December, we celebrate Posada (a Mexican Christmas tradition about the coming of the three kings). As part of Sunday morning worship, we occasionally involve a Korean fan-dance team composed of women from three different nationalities. Look for innovative ways to celebrate and to promote a spirit of inclusion in your church.

Form Strategic Missions Partnerships

FBC Duluth has established strategic missions and church-planting partnerships in countries heavily represented in the Duluth population and by the diverse people of our church. Currently we are planting churches in India and Mexico and hope to be planting a church in Nigeria soon. These partnerships are helping us accomplish several cross-cultural goals in pursuit of our own transition to living color:

- They foster greater sensitivity toward other cultures and more specifically those represented among us by encouraging everyone to participate (in one way or another) in extending the love of God to diverse people groups.

- They communicate our genuine respect and a concern for native homelands to the diverse people worshipping as one in our church and living in our shared community.

- They promote a "glocal" vision for our congregation. This past year we took our first ever cross-cultural team on mission trip (participants were from four different birth nations).[9]

Though our own journey is not yet complete, great things continue to happen at FBC Duluth. May God continue to bless us, and you, in seeking to become a healthy, multiethnic community of faith.

re:MIX Terminology

To transition your church to living color will require not only new terminology but also a rephrasing of existing vocabulary.

Multiethnic

Michael O. Emerson reports,

> Research on a variety of organizations has shown that it takes 20 percent or more of another group to have their voices heard and effect cultural change on an organization. Short of that percentage, people are largely tokens. Part of this 20 percent or more rule is mathematics. At 20 percent of another group, the probability of contact across the groups is 99 percent. For these reasons, I define a [multiethnic] congregation as one having less than 80 percent of any single racial group.[10]

A healthy multiethnic church is defined not only by the diversity of its attending members but also by the following:

- diversity of both paid and lay leadership
- broad acceptance of various styles of programming and worship
- health of cross-cultural relationships among its members
- cross-cultural competence exhibited by its leaders

The desire to build a healthy multiethnic church is like the journey toward sanctification: something that requires patient and purposeful pursuit over time. With this in mind, we should not think that a church has ever fully arrived. In transitioning a church to living color, then, leaders should take it one step at a time by asking the following questions, and acting upon them:

- What do we believe theologically?
- What do we embrace philosophically?
- What can we do practically?
- When can we do it realistically?[11]

35

Missional

Bob Whitesel wrote in *Organix*, "To speak of being *missional* is to speak of acquainting and reconciling people with God through faith in Jesus Christ before, during, and after their conversion."[12]

- The term *missional* can be used to describe individuals and churches that actively participate in the mission of God by advancing his will and kingdom on earth as it is in heaven.
- "The missional church knows that [it] must be a cross-cultural missionary (contextual) people and adopt a missionary stance in relation to [its] community."[13]

Mission

Author David J. Bosch notes, "Mission is not primarily an activity of the church, but *an attribute of God.* Indeed, God is a missionary God."[14]

Mission and the Church

According to William H. Willimon,

- "It is the nature of this God to reach out; thus the chief defining characteristic of the gospel is *relentless reach* (1 Thessalonians 2:1, 8, 9; Romans 1:1)."[15]
- "God has a gregarious determination to draw all things unto Himself (John 12:23); this is His mission. Therefore, the church exists not for itself but rather to signal and embody God's intentions for the whole world."[16]
- "God is going to redeem what belongs to Him; and His primary means of accomplishing this is the church."[17]

Mission and the Christian

- Christ-followers have been commissioned to serve and support God in accomplishing His mission (Matt 28:19-20).
- Christ-followers have been *entrusted* with God's message of reconciliation (2 Cor 5:19).
- Christ-followers are ambassadors for Christ (2 Cor 5:20).

Missio Dei

Theologians have used the term *missio Dei* (Latin, "mission of God") to describe God's active pursuit of fallen humanity in reconciling us to himself.[18]

- "The *missio Dei* is 'God on mission' to reintroduce Himself [to] His wayward offspring and restore true fellowship."[19]

- "*Missio Dei* describes the grand mission of God because only He can accomplish it. . . . [Thus] Christians actively participate in the *missio Dei* having been called and equipped for the extraordinary task of reconnecting people to a loving, seeking Father."[20]

Living on Mission (Missional Living)

Living on mission requires actions and choices by Christian churches and Christ-centered individuals that point to God as the source and reason for our actions before, during, and even after conversion.[21]

Christian churches living on mission respond daily to the question:

What can we do to serve others today to demonstrate the Father's love and his desire to be reunited with those who do not yet know him as we do, or those in need of growing in their relationship with him?

- **Pre-evangelism:** a Christian church establishes a program to serve the needs of young people aging out of the foster-care system.

- **Evangelism:** a Christian church reaches out and warmly embraces teen mothers, shares the gospel with them, and provides ongoing love and material support, leading many of them to receive Christ, be baptized, and become congregation members.

- **Discipleship:** a Christian church leads its people to embrace the multiethnic vision and transition to living color for the sake of the gospel.

Christ-centered individuals living on mission respond daily to the question:

What can I do to serve others today to demonstrate the Father's love and his desire to be reunited with those who do not yet know him as I do, or those in need of growing in their relationship with him?

- **Pre-evangelism**: a Christ-centered businessperson establishes a program for Rwandan scholars and mobilizes universities in the United States to admit them on scholarship.

- **Evangelism**: a Christ-centered former madam begins rescuing women from sex trafficking and drug abuse, leading prostitutes to Christ and bringing them with her to church.

- **Discipleship**: a Christ-centered dentist begins providing weekly free cleanings to residents in an underserved community.

Developmental Strategy

Put Others First

Speaking to the church at Philippi, Paul writes, "Instead of each person watching out for their own good, watch out for what is better for others" (Phil 2:4). Notice the verse is not written to an individual, but collectively, to a church. A church must look out not only for its own needs—that is, the needs of its majority membership—but also, and more importantly, for the needs of those members less represented in number, responsibility, or authority. In part it must do so by practicing accommodation not assimilation, by empowering diverse leaders, and by promoting a spirit of inclusion.[22]

Beyond this, it must also advance the *missio Dei* and seek to meet the needs of diverse others in the community whether they are or are not yet believers. Only in so doing will their light so shine in a way that reflects God's love for all people in an authentic and attractive way (Matt 5:16).

A church of living color, therefore, in the words of Saint Francis of Assisi, will not so much seek to be understood, but to understand; not so much to be heard, but to listen; not so much to be loved, but to love.[23]

Pastor the Community

When people of different cultures in a community have a need, do they think first of your church? Wouldn't you want them to do so?

Toward that end, leaders in a church of living color should not see themselves merely as pastors of a church but as pastors to their communities. In creating a church that reflects the community, mission will no longer be for your church a program; rather, mission will become who you are and what you're all about. You will not have to go beyond the membership to see or understand the needs of the community; the people, the members of such a church themselves, *are* the community! As you help your own you will be helping the community: for as you help your own they will inevitably tell others within their spheres of influence about *their* church, its heart for all people, and before long the community at large will turn to your church in time of need.

Provide for Diverse Needs

By creating a church of living color—one that is more reflective of changing demographics in a community and more broadly of society as a whole—paid and lay leaders will become increasingly aware of the needs of diverse others in and outside the congregation. Once such needs are realized and understood, leadership should mobilize to meet them in a cross-culturally competent way.

Of course, you will not likely encounter the needs of diverse others sitting behind a desk or by talking with others like yourself. Multiethnic church leaders are engaged in and always listening to the community in order to develop cross-cultural relationships and competence. In such a way, providing for the needs of diverse others is developed from the ground up.[24]

By organizing to meet such needs, whether through church-based programs or by creating an umbrella nonprofit focused on the community (as Mark has done at Mosaic Church in Little Rock and as we'll discuss in chapter 4), your church will expand its breadth of influence, engender goodwill in the community, and gain favor with the people.

Partner for Progress

You can expedite the transition to living color, and with it opportunities for your church to expand its breadth of influence, by partnering with existing ethnic churches or organizations serving the needs of the community. You shouldn't view the size of your church or budget or location as limiting factors to community engagement. Your church may be geographically far removed from the systemic issues of race and class, but that should not obstruct your sincere investment in cross-cultural community engagement. The fact is, churches and organizations in underserved communities are in great need of your attention, encouragement, and investment.

In pursuit of partnership, avoid condescension. Keep in mind that your way is just *a* way, not necessarily *the* way to engage the community. Approach those already in the space with humility, a desire first and foremost to listen, to learn, and to serve. If you are establishing governing leadership, invite need-meeting organizations to share responsible authority with the church, to shape future direction, and to sit on your board(s).

With this in mind, send the church as well as its money. Since the *missio Dei* involves reconciliation, personal encounter is necessary to transition your church to living color and subsequently impact a diverse community. Cross-cultural and organizational partnerships create opportunities for both intentional and organic relationships from which a desire to share assets, finances, and volunteers will flow quite naturally.

In Greater Boston, for example, multiple churches are engaged with one another and serving cross-culturally to advance mission. Pastor Dana Baker, who lives and serves there, shares seven values that govern and guide this multiple church partnership:

1. Prayer

2. Diversity

3. Collaboration

4. Innovation

5. Boston-Reaching

6. Gospel-Centered

7. Hope[25]

Pursue Your Own Metrics

As we mentioned in the introduction, for nearly fifty years the American church has measured success by numbers, dollars, and buildings. Like it or not, pastors know this to be true. Questions that begin with the words "How many . . . ?" and "How big . . . ?" are ones we commonly face, must answer, or otherwise discuss on a daily basis. Younger, less established, or new-to-ministry pastors are the ones most likely to feel pressure to perform in this regard. Similarly, pastors of smaller churches bear the burden of microaggressions that often, though unintentionally, suggest their ministries are not as significant, noteworthy, or instructive as those within larger churches—those pastors most likely to be invited onto the main stage, to write a book, or to address their denomination at the annual meeting.

In fact, for all the talk of launching big and growing even faster, we've come to realize that explosive church growth more often than not leads to internal focus.[26] This is why the very ones Jesus looked in the eye and said, "Go . . ." stayed. That's right! Peter, James, and John, along with the rest of the apostles, stayed in Jerusalem, in spite of the Great Commission.

Why, you ask?

Look, as much as I (Mark) might love for Mosaic Church in Little Rock to grow beyond our current attending membership, if three thousand people came to Christ and joined our church in Little Rock tomorrow, our entire leadership team would be freaking out. "We don't have enough parking! We don't have enough nursery space! We need more bathrooms!" they would say. More significantly, there would be so many immediate needs requiring our time and attention, we wouldn't need to look or go anywhere else for years to come. Surely something similar happened in Jerusalem, and to the disciples, as the church there exploded in growth following Peter's first public sermon in Acts 2. For such reasons, throughout the New Testament, we don't find the disciples venturing very far, or some ever at all, beyond Jerusalem, in spite of the fact that Jesus looked them in the eye and said, "Go" (Matt 28:19).

It's important for you to understand, then, as a pastor transitioning your church to living color, that the value of your church in the community or in the kingdom of God is not tied to the size of Sunday morning attendance. Nor is Sunday morning attendance the definitive measure of your church. For instance, when answering the question of size, can I (Mark) count the additional sixteen hundred people a month (approximately 375 a week) that our church serves on Tuesdays that receive from us three to four full days of healthy meals each month? In other words, it's not homogeneous size on Sunday but breadth of community and kingdom impact throughout the rest of the week that is, in our view, a more significant measure of a church's significance and success.

Churches seeking to re:MIX think outside the box, then, and develop their own metrics of success. They do so driven by a recognition that changing demographics and needs in their own communities provide a unique opportunity to advance social justice and benevolent good in fulfillment of Matthew 5:16.[27]

Garfield Memorial (United Methodist Church) • Cleveland, Ohio

To Win Some from Every Kind of People

Pastor Chip Freed

Over the years, Garfield Memorial has become a well-established UMC in Cleveland. Similar to many traditional mainline churches at the turn of the century, however, we knew something was wrong, given thirty years of declining membership, attendance, and children's ministry participation. In 2004, the makeup of the congregation was 99 percent white, and most attendees lived in affluent neighborhoods.

In response, at the end of that year, we initiated a culture shift on three fronts:

1. We determined to become an outward-focused church.

2. We renewed our commitment to the Great Commission.

3. We embraced a calling to become multiethnic and economically diverse.

To support the turnaround, we then implemented structural change through:

A New Statement of Purpose

We wrote a new vision statement, clarifying new values, which read: "Garfield Memorial is a **safe** place to search and **grow** in faith in a very **authentic** way amidst a **diverse** community of all people-groups. We are not a perfect church, therefore we will be a community of the non-offensive and unoffended, and offer and practice **forgiveness** wherever it is required."

An Enhanced Worship Experience

We enlisted highly competent worship leaders to offer a high-quality experience on Sunday mornings and to present a variety of music to which a diverse and unchurched audience could easily connect.

42

A Diverse Leadership Team

We began to hire and otherwise empower diverse leaders to represent the increasingly diverse community in which the church existed and sought to minister.

As a result of these decisions, Garfield Memorial began again to flourish, and we have continued to grow over the last ten years. For example, in 2004, in the nearly all-white congregation, there were approximately 450 active members, with 200 regularly attending Sunday morning worship and only 15 participating in children's ministry. Today the church has some 1,100 active members, with over 600 people attending worship each week and 150 children participating on two campuses. More than this, Garfield Memorial is now known as one of the most multiethnic, economically diverse churches in Ohio! It is a church in which the largest single ethnic group comprises no more than 52 percent of the congregation. Because of our ethnic and economic diversity and witness, we are having a major impact in the city of Cleveland, to the glory of God.

Within our own denomination, too, we are helping to change attitudes and understanding. For instance, most of the multiethnic and economically diverse churches that do exist in the United Methodist Church are located in downtown or urban settings. In these churches, members from the suburbs choose to drive in to the city in order to be on mission with the poor. What's different about Garfield Memorial, however, is that the church is located in a highly affluent suburban area of Cleveland, and it's the urban poor who are commuting in order to be part of our unique community of faith. This has not only caught the attention of denominational leaders but suggests that churches in the suburbs, like ours, can and should transition to living color for the sake of multiethnic and missional advance in an increasingly diverse society.

Conclusion

Like the Apostle Paul in 1 Corinthians 9:19-23, Garfield Memorial has determined to become all things to all people that by all means it might win some from every kind: black and white, wealthy and poor, old and young. Through structural shifts, strategic marketing, community engagement, random acts of kindness, and intentional mission, the church has become as diverse as the community it seeks to reach and save with a message of God's love for all people. Like fishermen in the New Testament, it has thrown out its net on the east side of Cleveland, looking not only for one kind of fish, but for a diverse array of fish within a fifteen- to twenty-mile radius of its facility. For the sake of the gospel, your church can and should do the same.

Chapter 3

▍: Create an *Inclusive* Community of Faith

Conduct yourselves with all humility, gentleness, and patience.
Accept each other with love, and make an effort to preserve the unity
of the Spirit with the peace that ties you together.
—Ephesians 4:2-3

Growing Awareness

Since the publication of the books *Divided by Faith* (2000) and *Building a Healthy Multi-Ethnic Church* (2007), growing awareness of the need, opportunities, and ways to develop healthy multiethnic churches has risen sharply. In addition, the Mosaix Global Network has helped advance interest by hosting local and regional gatherings, as well as two national gatherings (to date), including the first national conference of the subject attended by four hundred leaders from thirty-one states in San Diego, California (November 2010). At Mosaix's second national conference in Long Beach, California (November 2013), just over one thousand were involved. Through such means and more, the number of pastors seeking additional understanding has steadily increased over the past fifteen years, as has receptivity to the message. The fact that you hold this book in your hand helps make the point. Thus, there is a growing number of churches that have reached at least 20 percent diversity in their attending membership, as cited in chapter 1. This number is expected to grow exponentially in the next five to ten years. In fact, since 2005, Mosaix has championed a vision to see 20 percent of churches in the United States achieve 20 percent diversity by the year 2020. From the looks of things, the growing movement may hit that mark.

Of course, there is so much more to becoming and measuring the health of a vibrant church of living color than mere percentages reveal. For this reason, be encouraged: you're on the right path, and you're not alone.

Unintended Consequences

Sociologist Michael O. Emerson, coauthor of *Divided by Faith*, has identified four unintended consequences of systemically segregated churches:

1. They reproduce inequality.

2. They encourage oppression.

3. They strengthen racial division.

4. They heighten political separation.[1]

Think not? Consider just one example to support these claims. Research conducted on more than two hundred thousand churches in the United States by David T. Olson, author of *The American Church in Crisis*, found that between 2000 and 2009:

- The growth rate in evangelical churches with a zip code in which Anglos made up more than 80 percent of the population grew by an average of 3.5 percent. Those with a zip code where Anglos made up less than 80 percent of the population declined by an average of 1.9 percent.[2]

- The growth rate in evangelical churches with a median income of more than sixty thousand dollars was 17.6 percent. Those with a median income of less than thirty thousand dollars declined by 4.3 percent.[3]

- The growth rate in evangelical churches with a median education level beyond high school grew by an average of 4.3 percent. Churches with a median education level twelfth grade and under declined by an average of 2.7 percent.[4]

A New Testament Expectation

Promoting a spirit of inclusion within the local church is necessary for pastors seeking to be biblical, credible, and responsible with the gospel of Jesus Christ. As one of seven core commitments of a healthy multiethnic church, it is also a New Testament expectation.[5] Thus, the concept of inclusion is not new to our time and culture; nor is the struggle for believers to be one in the church for the sake of the gospel.

Consider and learn from just a few biblical passages that demonstrate the challenges early church leaders also faced in wrestling with such concerns:

Don't Make It Difficult for Diverse Others to Belong

Some people came down from Judea teaching the family of believers, "Unless you are circumcised according to the custom we've received from Moses, you can't be saved." Paul and Barnabas took sides against these Judeans and argued strongly against their position. . . . The apostles and the elders gathered to consider this matter. . . . [James said,] "Therefore, I conclude that we shouldn't create problems for Gentiles who turn to God." (Acts 15:1-2, 6, 19)

Don't Attend to Some over Others Based on Race or Ethnicity

But when Cephas came to Antioch, I opposed him to his face, because he was wrong. He had been eating with the Gentiles before certain people came from James. But when they came, he began to back out and separate himself, because he was afraid of the people who promoted circumcision. And the rest of the Jews also joined him in this hypocrisy so that even Barnabas got carried away with them in their hypocrisy. (Gal 2:11-13)

Don't Extend Privilege to Some over Others Based on Class or Status

My brothers and sisters, when you show favoritism you deny the faithfulness of our Lord Jesus Christ, who has been resurrected in glory. Imagine two people coming into your meeting. One has a gold ring and fine clothes, while the other is poor, dressed in filthy rags. Then suppose that you were to take special notice of the one wearing fine clothes, saying, "Here's an excellent place. Sit here." But to the poor person you say, "Stand over there"; or, "Here, sit at my feet." Wouldn't you have shown favoritism among yourselves and become evil-minded judges? (James 2:1-4)

A Modern-Day Challenge

Christians will use many reasons to justify the continued segregation (some prefer the term *separation*) of "their" church along the lines of race, class, and culture. Each in its own way makes sense and is otherwise a natural response. Nevertheless, we cannot forget or set aside the fact that believers have been called to go above and beyond what is otherwise natural to live, learn, and love in the supernatural: to lay down preferences; set aside worries, doubts, and fears; forgive and be reconciled to one another; and to exercise faith, courage, and sacrifice, all in pursuit of what the Lord otherwise requires of us collectively, and not just individually.

Here are just a few of the more common excuses for maintaining the status quo, and how you might address each of them when attempting to articulate the re:MIX vision:

Involvement Overseas

For decades, many churches have extended themselves faithfully, sacrificially, and cross-culturally across the oceans. We are not at all suggesting they cease from doing so. But today, as Pastor David Boyd has observed, "You don't have to cross an ocean to reach the world."[6] Therefore, we should ask: Are these same churches willing to extend themselves cross-culturally as well, right here at home, across the street? If so, how so? If not, why not; and more significantly, what does this suggest? How will an increasingly diverse community interpret the lack of engagement?

Birds of a Feather

In nature there is safety in numbers. When animals of a similar kind group together, it helps deter predators. But we are not animals; nor should we be motivated by fear of others different from ourselves. Rather, the church should be moved to love others as we love ourselves (our own). Sadly, it's fear of others that drives racism and injustice in our world today. It always has; perhaps in the world it always will. But we are not of this world; therefore, we must not give in to such fear of others or allow it to inform the church. Remember, "perfect love casts out fear" (1 John 4:18 NRSV).

Historic Mistrust

Throughout US history, a government dominated by white power and privilege often sought the cooperation of other people groups only to later renege on contracts, rewrite the rules, or otherwise breach trust once agreements were reached. This was particularly true in its dealings with Native Americans and African Americans. Embedded in our culture, then, is a historic mistrust among minorities of white culture, in general, when it suggests coming together "for the good of everyone." Rather than deny or defend past realities, white pastors should acknowledge them. Only then can conversations move to deeper levels of transparency, trust be established, and any mistrust diffused.

Perpetuating Culture

In Australia, there are a great number of clubs that have been formed around specific people groups and cultures. For instance, there is the German Austrian Club in Cabramatta; the King Tom Croatian Club in Edensor Park; the Russian Club in Strathfield; and the Rembrandt Dutch Club (RDC) in St Marys. According to the Russian Club's website, it all started in 1924 when expatriates "wanted to have the means of getting together in some place where they could speak their language and have opportunity to fulfill their needs to retain cultural identity."[7] The Rembrandt Dutch Club's aim is "to keep the Dutch traditions going within the Australian community—to please the older generation, but at the same time teach the younger ones about the food, drink, and (our) party habits."[8] In other words, if you want to perpetuate culture, start a club; that's not the mission of the church, at least not as defined in the New Testament.

Creating a Cross Culture

More often than not, those who are not part of the majority culture in a particular church must check their own cultures at the door if they are to be accepted by the congregation. As Dr. Rodney L. Cooper says, in such situations minorities must "go along to get along."[9] Generally speaking, people typically want to make others look, behave, and act like themselves. Missiologists call this the "Creator Complex." C. Peter Wagner once noted, "Deep in the heart of humans, even in missionaries, lurks a *Creator Complex* by which [we] delight in making other people over in [our] own image."[10] Such attitudes and desires, however, are not helpful, nor will they help you transition a church of living color.

On the other hand, to re:MIX the church is not at all to suggest that people must give up their cultural identity or distinctions in order to make it work. If so, the resulting "stew" would taste bland. Human culture and cultural identity is important, for sure. It is to be respected, maintained, and passed on. It grounds, informs, and enlightens. But our passion for human culture must always remain subject to the culture of heaven, the culture of the cross. As the old song says:

> Blest be the tie that binds, our hearts in Christian love;
> The fellowship of kindred minds is like to that above.[11]

With such things in mind, and in order to create an inclusive community of faith, the responsibility lies more with those in the majority than it does with those in the minority to will themselves to:

- *adjust* its attitudes and actions;
- *adapt* existing cultural forms that may unintentionally create obstacles to inclusion;
- *add* new cultural forms and expressions of faith.

According to the Apostle Paul, apart from the inclusion of varying cultures in the local church, we will not "have the power to [fully] grasp love's width and length, height and depth, together with all believers" (Eph 3:18). In other words, believers from each culture, as well as each culture itself, embody a unique expression of the Father and bring distinctive aspects of just who God is to the table. Only together, then, can we get beyond an experience with God informed to some degree by our own cultural perspectives to a place in which the church is "filled entirely with the fullness of

50

God" (v. 19). This was Paul's prayer and expectation for the multiethnic church at Ephesus. It remains God's desire and hope for us today (John 17:23).

re:MIX Considerations

The research of Michael O. Emerson and Christian Smith, published in *Divided by Faith*, suggests that the more involved people are in evangelical churches, the fewer friends they have outside of church and the less overall time they spend with people besides their church friends. According to Emerson, most Christians are not only racially segregated from one another but also relationally segregated.[12]

Proximity to one another, however, can help us develop crosscultural relationships of transparency and trust. This in turn leads to the crosscultural understanding and competence needed to overcome prejudice. Working in close contact is one of the best ways to grow in knowledge, understanding, and respect for someone from another culture (proximity breeds acceptance).[13]

Ongoing and intentional effort, however, will be needed. According to Dr. Rodney L. Cooper, "Exposure does not mean acceptance. Insight does not guarantee change."[14]

Northwood Church (Southern Baptist Convention) • Keller, Texas

Value Humanity over Homogeneity

Pastor Bob Roberts

It was the world that caused me to become intentional in leading Northwood to engage people of ethnic and economic diversity living in our community. I began to ask myself: How can I rightly extend the love of Christ to the people of Vietnam, to Muslims, Arabs, and Jews, to followers of Buddha, to Communists, and a whole host of others across the oceans, yet not love similar ones across the street from my church?

It wasn't that we didn't love diverse people in our community, or that others who were different from us were not welcome at Northwood. Rather, I came to understand the significant difference between diverse others being part of our church and feeling as if it is their church.

There was also the fact that the majority of the population in Keller has traditionally been Anglo—80 percent, in fact. But rather than use this as an excuse, I began to consider the other 20 percent of the population.

So we decided to re:MIX.

With all of our global work and experience behind us, I assumed it would be a piece of cake. I also assumed that no one would question our intentions. Oh I was wrong! Here's what I learned about us in the process of our church transitioning to living color.

People of other races were welcome at Northwood in the past, as long as they liked us; that is, as long as they liked the way we did things. In other words, to the degree that others were willing to assimilate in becoming like us, all was and would be well. Sadly, I came to realize we were unintentionally asking people to leave their ethnicities and cultures at the door in order to be one with us at Northwood. Of course, this was never spoken and honestly we didn't even realize it for quite some time. To say "We want you" was to suggest, "We want you to be like us."

When we began to be more intentional, then, we had to make room not just for color but also for culture, and that was challenging. Over time, the value of humanity has become more important to us than the value of homogeneity.

Yet make no mistake: people have voted with their feet. It seems that people from the majority culture are fine as long as those from other cultures are only sitting beside them in the pews. But when diverse people are appointed to leadership positions over them? For some folks, sadly, it's just too hard to submit to someone of a different (minority) background. Has it been worth the effort, however, losing some to gain and empower diverse others? You bet it has! Any church that desires credibility in today's society cannot ignore the issues and complexity of race and still expect to be heard or respected.

For those now transitioning churches to living color, I suggest:

1. Read the writings of multiethnic church leaders such as Efrem Smith, Mark DeYmaz, Soong-Chan Rah, David Anderson, and Bryan Lorrits.

2. Visit at least two churches pursuing transition in an area similar to your own community, even if you have to fly to another state.

3. Share regularly about what you're learning, seeing, and thinking with the staff and elder board or leadership council.

4. Preach about God loving the whole world, about how migration is changing the face of the world, about the unique opportunity we have today to open our church to people living in our communities from all races, ethnicities, and nations.

5. Focus on diversifying your elder board or leadership council so they can be involved with identifying and hiring more diverse leaders.

6. Get a mentor or coach to walk with you through transition.[15]

7. Elevate the value of becoming one in Christ as more important than simply growing the church as much as possible, filled with only one race or ethnicity, otherwise isolated from the world and the greater body of Christ.

Three Types of Cultural Adapters

Inclusion begins by understanding that people have different views on how much of their culture they want to preserve and how much of it they are willing to release. To appreciate different people, even within the same culture, a church of living color makes all three types of cultural adapters feel welcome.[16]

1. *Consonant Adapters* are people who adapt almost entirely to another culture.

   o Over time they will mirror the other culture in their conduct, dress, and ways of thinking.

   o They will usually navigate their way into a church of a different culture.

2. *Selective Adapters* are people who adapt to some parts of another culture but reject other aspects.[17]

   o Though they want to preserve their cultural heritage they will compromise in many areas to preserve harmony.

   o They often attend diverse churches with blended worship, because they like the harmony amid the diversity. Because they prefer harmony, however, they may often avoid tackling challenging cultural issues.

3. *Dissonant Adapters* are people who have a strong loyalty to their culture and yearn to preserve its traditions in the face of a dominant culture's power.

   o Dissonant adapters may reject weekly blended worship because they prefer a worship expression that preserves more of their cultural traditions. They want diversity, but they also want to teach others about their culture and to gain a respect for it.

   o They will prefer churches that have multiple and diverse worship expressions.[18]

Five Key Areas for Inclusion

In transitioning a church to living color, the following five areas will likely raise the most concern within the body.

Worship

In Ephesians 6:10-13, the Apostle Paul warns that our struggle to be one in the church for the sake of the gospel is not waged among flesh and blood—by which he means the color of one's skin (flesh) and cultural heritage (blood)—upon which so many churches today have been established and remain divided to the detriment of our unity and witness (John 13:35).

Perhaps there is no better place to showcase a church's heart and commitment to inclusion than in its weekly gathering. As one pastor said, "Each month we try to sing an even distribution of contemporary Christian music, gospel music, and urban praise. Of course, doing this with excellence is easier with talented musicians and a motivated congregation, but I believe every church can do something."[19] This is especially true when you keep in mind that inclusive worship involves more than a song, a band, or musical style. Do you share the pulpit regularly with others of different ethnicities? How diverse are the Communion servers, scripture readers, or those who pray before the body? Who is entrusted with collecting the offering? These and more questions should be considered and addressed in seeking to promote a spirit of inclusion through worship.

Points to consider:

- The past experience, personalities, or preferences of one group over another must not be allowed to dictate to the church the terms of its worship.

- Include more than one language on slides being used in the service by (a) preparing slides earlier in the week to allow time for translation, and (b) using fewer lyrics per slide.

- Allow people to pray in their heart language at times without requiring translation in order to "comprehend, with all the saints, what is the breadth and length and height and depth, and to know the love of Christ that surpasses knowledge" (Eph 3:18-19 NRSV).

Leadership

Sadly, the American church has had a poor record through the years of inclusive leadership. A young African American pastor put it this way: "They [white Christians] want you in their churches, but they won't let you on their leadership committees."[20]

Empowering diverse leaders, therefore, is essential to the establishment of an authentic church of living color. In describing the multiethnic church at Antioch, for example, Luke points this out by listing its leadership not only by name but also by country of origin (Acts 13:1; see also Acts 4:36; 9:11). In addition, Paul models intentionality in the choosing (hiring) of Timothy (Acts 16:1). Timothy was not only biracial (having a Jewish mother and a Greek father) but "the brothers and sisters in Lystra and Iconium spoke well of him" (Acts 16:2).

In other words, we're not talking about token hires, or diversity for diversity's sake. Rather, it's about creating an inclusive team of diverse individuals who mutually and joyfully share responsibility for the direction and development of the church, from the pulpit to the nursery and at every stop in between. In so doing, a diverse leadership team, including both lay and paid leaders, will demonstrate what is not only expected in terms of cross-cultural relationships and partnership within the body, but what is possible.

Points to consider:

- People looking to validate any claim that a church is authentically inclusive will first look at the church's website and more specifically, pictures and titles on its leadership page.
- "Intentionality [in regard to empowering diverse leaders] . . . [is] the middle ground between quota and wishful thinking.[21]
- To increase the pool of minority candidates who are ready, eager, and able to serve, churches and denominations must rethink traditional credentialing, time requirements, and financial burdens, largely developed by and with the majority culture (whites) in mind.

Language

It should both comfort and challenge you to know that the very first church on earth faced and overcame obstacles in uniting diverse believers speaking different languages (Acts 6:1-6). In so doing, existing majority leadership:

- *realized* that certain ones within the church were being overlooked largely due to language;
- *recognized* it was important to find a solution;
- *responded* by empowering leaders from within the overlooked group to help meet the needs.

If they did it, so can we!

That said, there is not necessarily a one-size-fits-all way to overcome the obstacles in providing effective ministry to people speaking two or more languages in one church. Indeed there are intrinsic pros and cons to varying approaches. Some churches do not provide a service for a separate language but offer translation of their service via headsets. Others provide separate language services but must avoid becoming two churches under one roof in perception or reality. Still others facilitate two or more specific language venues simultaneously on Sunday morning so that children and youth can be integrated in one program.

Points to consider:

- The important thing is not so much the way you are doing it at any given time but that you try, learn, and try again, refining your approach over time based on current or changing context.

- Signal to the public that you welcome, expect, and include others who do not speak English by using signage both in and outside the church that reflects two or more languages. Likewise, ensure that weekly bulletins, electronic newsletters, and websites are also available in these languages and properly translated.

- While translation is helpful, first-generation congregants should not be expected to pray or be excluded from praying in their heart language. For often in such moments, "the same Spirit agrees with our spirit, that we are God's children" (Rom 8:16).

Resources

Authentic churches of living color provide for the fair use and allocation of resources, including facilities (space), time, and money, without partiality (Acts 10:34). According to Dr. John M. Perkins, such sharing of resources without strings attached fosters trust, cooperation, and competence across demographic lines. In addition, he suggests that racial reconciliation is best facilitated when those with accumulated means share with those who are less fortunate.[22]

With this in mind, the sharing of church resources based upon need and not extraneous factors such as history, convenience, or for that matter, inconvenience, fosters a sense of physical and emotional inclusion: this church is not *yours* but *ours*. An inclusive church, then, ensures that each cultural group shares equally in the benefits of wealth accumulation despite specific attendance numbers or financial contributions coming from varying demographic groups.

Points to consider:

- Avoid creating two or more churches operating independently from one another under the same roof.

- Ensure that each culture has equal access and opportunity to take advantage of such things as rooms, times, and finances, despite specific attendance numbers or contributions.

- Include diverse others in the decision-making process as it pertains to the allocation of resources.

Planning

It's a sobering reality: every pastor is an interim pastor. The church you pastor today will likely look very different in the future, for better or worse. Therefore prudent pastors not only plan for the present but as best they can they position the church for the future. Failure to consider, to involve, or to hire minority leaders today with the future in mind will likely lead to frustrated efforts in seeking to engage rapidly changing communities and urban complexities down the road.

Inclusive leaders are students of change; and more than this, they are lifelong learners recognizing that cultures and communities continue to evolve. Fortunately for us, and more than at any other time in human history, the Internet allows good planners to chart current demographics and forecast future trends in a specific community.[23]

Points to consider:

- As part of present and future planning, include leaders who represent growing diversity in the community and not just those who reflect the current situation.

- In order to earn relational trust and professional respect, listen to minority leaders without assumption. Learn from them; don't instruct them. Include them; don't inform them.

- As you discuss possibilities with diverse others on your team, keep in mind that your way is just *a* way of doing things, and not necessarily "the" way that things should be done.

St. Paul's (United Methodist Church) • Asheville, North Carolina

From Exciting Concept to Joyful Practice

Pastor In-Yong Lee

Our re:MIX began when I attended a seminar in Charlotte, North Carolina, March 1–2, 2013. St. Paul's UMC in Asheville was seeking ways in which to transition given the changing demographics of our community. Of the many seminars I have attended, this one articulated the vision I was seeking. I returned to share my passion for transition with the Administrative Council (AC), the church's governing body, and soon together we studied *Building a Healthy Multi-Ethnic Church*. Afterward, the AC decided that St. Paul's would intentionally transition into a church of living color, a multiethnic church, and the new vision was shared with and later embraced by the whole congregation.

I then joined a coaching group sponsored by Mosaix with four other pastors from our denominational conference. The five churches meet monthly via the Internet with our coach and for peer-to-peer learning along the way. From these sessions I have discovered many new and promising practices that have helped us turn passion into reality at St. Paul's.

Although the church had been predominantly white, it had long become known for its openness to including minorities. In fact it was one of only a few historically white churches in Asheville known to welcome nonwhite people, as evidenced by the stained-glass window featuring ethnically diverse children with Jesus. Even more, the people of St. Paul's welcomed me, an Asian

59

female, as their pastor in 2007, and they have continued to love and support me ever since.

Over the past three years we have experienced wonderful success in pursuit of our goal. Here are just eight things we have done and benefited from along the re:MIX way:

1. We used *The Multi-Ethnic Christian Life Primer* to establish the vision within our church.

2. We applied for and received a ten-thousand-dollar Racial and Ethnic Local Church Grant from the UMC General Board of Global Ministries. With the grant, we started providing simultaneous translation in Spanish and Korean during our worship services.

3. We asked Duke Divinity School to provide us with a Hispanic intern. Stacy Guinto-Salinas served from May 25 to August 3, and her internship was very helpful both for the congregation and for her, too, to grow in cross-cultural ministry competence.

4. We started a Spanish-speaking small group that meets monthly. Individuals first develop trusting, meaningful relationships within small groups, and then they extend those relationships to the larger body. Because of the cultural language barriers, different language groups can benefit from the small-group settings in which they can communicate in their own language and culture with some willing cross-cultural individuals among them. A Korean-speaking small group was also formed and launched in 2015.

5. We now annually conduct five cultural celebrations—African American (February), Irish (March), Native American (May), Hispanic (July), and Asian (November)—to raise cultural awareness in the congregation by learning to appreciate different cultural expressions of the same faith.

6. We started two English for Speakers of Other Languages classes at church in cooperation with the Asheville Literacy Council. I, too, have been learning Spanish, because it should be a two-way effort!

7. We began to emphasize the multiethnic nature of our church on the homepage of our website.

8. We began to advertise in a local Hispanic magazine, *Hola Carolina.*

Through all such efforts we have gained more ethnic members, which is wonderful, and improved the church's reputation in the community. Still, it will take time for others in the congregation to fully embrace the vision as it does in any existing homogeneous church. With this in mind, here's my advice:

Be patient.

Be persistent.

Persevere in prayer.

Conclusion

Churches can no longer ignore the systemic segregation of the local church if they hope to present a credible witness of Christlike love for all people in an increasingly diverse and cynical society. Rather, our churches must become inclusive communities of faith encouraging and embracing oneness in Christ across race and class distinctions. For he, himself, is our peace, having made us one through his own blood, and torn down dividing walls between us (Eph 2:14). Who are we to erect them again? Yes, the ground is level at the foot of the cross. It should be level in our churches as well.

Chapter 4

X: Create a *Transformative* Community of Faith

Let your light shine before people, so they can see the good things you do and [glorify] your Father who is in heaven.

—Matthew 5:16

In Matthew 28:19-20, commonly referred to as the Great Commission, Jesus commands his disciples, and therefore the church, to "go and make disciples of all nations" (Gr. *panta ta ethne*). He expects us to engage, evangelize, and equip as many people as possible from varying ethnic groups so that they, in turn, can reproduce the faith in others. As we discussed in chapter 3, it is no longer necessary to travel far for such purposes: the nations have come to live among us, alongside us, in close proximity to our churches. Indeed, we share the same neighborhoods. Therefore, by creating a reconciling, missional, and inclusive congregation, your church will be well positioned for the fourth and final aim of the re:MIX journey: to become a transformative community of faith, one that has a real and positive impact on its neighbors and its neighborhood; in the church, for sure, but also beyond its walls. To this collective, transformative engagement of community Christ calls the church.

As with the Great Commission Jesus similarly commissions the church to let its light shine in Matthew 5:16. Why? So that others may see our good works and glorify our Father in heaven. Let's break this down for a moment.

First, it is important to remind ourselves that Jesus is not speaking to an individual but to individuals collectively—a crowd of people. Given the rugged individualism of the West and our tendency to interpret every verse

63

in the Bible as speaking to "me," it is easy to lose sight of the fact that such commands and admonitions are more often than not spoken to a group. Thus it is expected that they will be fulfilled by a group working as one toward a common goal and with one purpose.

For example, Paul commands the multiethnic church at Ephesus to "lead a life worthy of the calling to which you [plural] have been called" (Eph 4:1 NRSV). From reading Ephesians 2–3, it is clear that their collective calling is to be one in the church for the sake of the gospel. In 4:2-3, Paul explains how they are to do so: by being humble, patient, gentle, loving, and diligent to preserve their unity. In 4:4-6 he explains why they are to do so: because there is one body and spirit; one hope, Lord, faith, and baptism; one God and Father of all (people) who is over all (people, working) through all (people), and in all (people).

With this in mind, and though the church technically had not yet been established, Christ instructs us in Matthew 5:16 to let our collective light shine before the community (as we'll discuss in a moment) by advancing good works. The Greek word for "good" is *kalos*, suggesting that the work is "excellent, admirable and commendable."[1] Through these commendable works, as recognized by those outside the church, namely, the community, light shines on our Father in heaven. In other words, God is lit up (glorified) for who he is and for all to see. In this way, individuals will be attracted to him, to the light, to the Lord, and to his church.

The ultimate objective of a re:MIX, then, is to prepare and position a church to have a more transformative effect on its increasingly diverse community. Like a spotlight that shines brightly in the night sky causing all who see it to wonder where it is and want to find it, so is a church whose good works in a community are fueled by an authentic, credible, tangible love for diverse others. Such light shines and attracts when churches pursue the following four good works and aims.[2]

1. Bless the Community

In becoming a church that reflects its community, a church will come to understand, intrinsically, the needs of its community. It will then be moved to meet these needs because of its close proximity to others in need. We're not so much talking here about location as we are about relationships. For instance, when the homeless and hungry become part of the church, the church will mobilize to provide food and clothing. Personal proximity and relational connection in and through the church produces genuine concern. When undocumented immigrants become part of the church, the church will become more sympathetic toward the plight of children affected by the decisions of adults—children they now love and serve personally in the nursery, through children's ministry, or in the youth group. And when teen mothers become part of that youth group, the church will be moved by compassion to help them with everything from diapers to free babysitting, so that they will stay in school, finish school, or complete a GED, increasing their chance of breaking cycles of poverty. These, in turn, will tell their friends where to find help and hope; at "my" church, they will say. Thus the community will be blessed by a church of living color, through the incarnational nature of its work, and relational connections to diverse people.

2. Lead People to Christ

Unless we engage and advance social justice in our communities, we cannot hope to see them transformed. Yet to pursue social justice in the community apart from addressing the spiritual needs of the community is to improve temporal conditions at the expense of eternal ones. Sadly, the American church tends to compartmentalize these ideals as if they are mutually exclusive. But they are not, nor should one be pitted against the other. To advance social justice as we've discussed is to shine a bright light on a God of love, grace, mercy, and hope. Such work is winsome for the gospel. But we dare not miss or neglect opportunities to close the deal—that is, to invite others to embrace Jesus Christ as their Lord and Savior. As we have already made clear, at the end of the day, this is our mission. Therefore, we should keep in mind that a transformative community of faith exists where Christ has fundamentally transformed lives.

3. Encourage the Greater Body

How can we authentically promote unity within our own church if we are unwilling to pray and partner with other churches throughout the city as well? Wherever competition still exists among pastors and churches in a city, it must be excised by pastors and churches willing to cooperate for the greater good. Pastors who re:MIX their churches are in a key position to forge cooperation. Their experience in bringing diverse people to the table,

65

recognizing their own way is a way and not necessarily the way to do things, and most importantly, having credibility as a peacemaker, all bode well for pastors wanting to extend themselves beyond their own denominations, network affiliations, and people groups, to others who share their love for God and the city. In the future, churches that work well together will thrive in the city together whereas those that isolate themselves will become increasingly irrelevant and marginalized.

4. Fulfill the Great Commission

Christ does not expect that we will be able to fulfill the Great Commission alone; we can only do so together. The collective possibilities are greatly enhanced when diverse believers go to the world as one in spirit and purpose, as we discussed earlier in this chapter. To create a transformative community of faith will require a change of thinking, being, and doing on the part of everyone involved. Regarding the vision and mission of the church, people must think differently: it's not so much about numbers, dollars, and buildings, as it is about the development of unity and diversity in the church, and its subsequent influence in the community. Who we are and are becoming must be informed by this vision as well. The good works we do, then, will point to God, attract others to our mission, and win respect in the community, all to the glory of our Father in heaven.

Crossover Church (Nondenominational) • Tampa, Florida

Think Like an Entrepreneur

Pastor "Urban D." Kyllonen

Crossover Church in Tampa went through an incredible season of growth. At our former campus we were bursting at the seams and doing three services without room to grow. So in 2010, we took a huge leap of faith. We leased a former Toys "R" Us store and repurposed the forty-three thousand square feet of dark space for expanded ministry in our target community: an urban area in Tampa called Suitcase City. Our young, innovative, multiethnic church continued to grow as we loved our neighbors and conducted outreach events in our needy community.

But something inside of me was unsettled. I knew we needed to do more than just give away backpacks and food. We needed not only to love our neighbors but somehow to empower them.

In 2012, I had lunch with the CEO of a local nonprofit, Community Development Corporation, and pitched the idea of potential partnership in pursuit of community transformation. I envisioned a program that would mentor families in crisis and ultimately seek to lift them out of poverty. He absolutely loved the idea! He returned to his office, put together a brochure, and launched a fund-raising campaign. Six months later, he had raised one hundred thousand dollars to help us open the program that now exists on his site and ours. For our part, we were able to hire two new part-time staff members to work with families in crisis from our church.

Since establishing the program, we have seen God do amazing things in rewriting the stories of entire families pulled out of dysfunction and given tools to pursue a healthy life. We have helped many find jobs and others set career goals that they are now working toward. Some have moved into better living conditions. One young man became the first person in his family ever to attend college. And we are helping men learn to lead their families by becoming better husbands and fathers. Two of our staff members are fully engaged and dedicated to this holistic discipleship.

Looking back on this part of our journey, I remember that our team had lots of great ideas for transforming the community, but we were stretched too thin to do anything. At points I thought there was nothing more we could do.

- We were a small staff running a large church with multiple layers of need and complexity.
- We didn't have the capacity to mentor families in crisis.
- We didn't have time to raise money or start another nonprofit to do it.

But with a mind-set of abundance, and believing God is faithful to provide for what he calls us to do (1 Thess 5:24), I overcame the obstacles by approaching a partner in pursuit of community transformation. Our partner was able to raise money, do the advance work, and establish our church as a host site. In time, Crossover has become the lead site, and our team's efforts have refined the program at our partner's site as well.

Today, our church works with over a dozen nonprofits in our zip code that meet different needs. We never duplicate or compete with other programs in our neighborhood. Instead we support one another and pull together to empower families. There may be existing programs in your own communities that you can work alongside.

However you go about it, remember:

- A church of living color is uniquely positioned to mobilize for impact in an increasingly diverse society.

- Empowerment is not an event; it's a lengthy process you must remain committed to over time.

- When you work in an urban, multiethnic, and economically diverse environment, the needs are increased and the resources are less. To engage them, think like an entrepreneur.

On Conversion and Community

"There is a danger that [homogeneous] congregations . . . become exclusive, arrogant, and racist. That danger must be resolutely combatted." —Donald A. McGavran[3]

"Social responsibility becomes an aspect not of Christian mission only, but also of Christian conversion. It is impossible to be truly converted to God without being thereby converted to our neighbor." —John R. W. Stott.[4]

"If conversion to Christianity makes no improvement in a man's outward actions—if he continues to be just as snobbish or spiteful or envious or ambitious

as he was before—then I think we must suspect that his 'conversion' was largely imaginary." —C. S. Lewis[5]

Beyond Cultural Bias

Of course, there is little hope of transitioning a church to living color, let alone of achieving measurable results in pursuit of community transformation, apart from deep-seated change that must first take place with the human heart. We're not talking about mere Christianity. Rather, following salvation and as a part of the sanctification process we must allow the Holy Spirit to work within us to overcome cultural bias rooted in past experience, personality, and preference. Indeed biases, particularly those related to race, class, or culture, are ingrained opinions learned and reinforced over time that hinder us from authentic relationships and unconditional acceptance of diverse others. Transformation of such prejudices requires more than mere external alteration; it requires attitudinal change that we are incapable of experiencing without God's help.

The Bible describes how Paul, a former oppressor of Christians, was transformed from his cultural bias and racially prejudiced attitudes. In describing his upbringing, Paul writes,

> If anyone else has reason to put their confidence in physical advantages, I have even more:
> I was circumcised on the eighth day.
> I am from the people of Israel and the tribe of Benjamin.
> I am a Hebrew of the Hebrews. . . .
> With respect to righteousness under the Law, I'm blameless. (Phil 3:4-6)

Notice, though, in describing his heart change following conversion, Paul writes,

> Our firm decision is to work from this focused center: One man died for everyone. That puts everyone in the same boat. He included everyone in his death so that everyone could also be included in his life, a resurrection life, a far better life than people ever lived on their own.
> Because of this decision we don't evaluate people by what they have or how they look. We looked at the Messiah that way once and got it all wrong, as you know. We certainly don't look at him that way anymore. Now we look inside, and what we see is that anyone united with the Messiah gets a fresh start, is created new. The old life is gone; a new life

69

burgeons! Look at it! All this comes from the God who settled the relationship between us and him, and then called us to settle our relationships with each other. (2 Cor 5:14-19 The Message)

In other words, at the "focused center" of the gospel message is the understanding that Christ died not just for the Jews, but for everyone else, too, so that all people could find a better life in him.

In this passage, Paul shares honestly about formerly evaluating people by what they had, how they looked, and how, following salvation, his perspective changed. Likewise, he expects that followers of Christ will give one another a fresh start relationally by not holding personal sin, cultural biases, or historical prejudices against each other. He explains that God models healing from estrangement and forgiveness of enemies.

We are thus called to follow God's lead in

- seeing people come to know God as we do through faith in Jesus Christ
- entering into loving, healthy relationships with one another without and beyond distinctions

A Helpful Tool

The Multi-Ethnic Christian Life Primer is the first daily devotional and small-group study focused on multiethnic life and church designed for people in the pews. Essentially, it's a tool for cross-cultural relationship and competence development rooted in biblical theology. Today, pastors seeking to re:MIX their churches are employing it with good success in their small-group systems and as part of a new members' enfolding process. In addition, church planters are using it to equip their leadership teams and establish small groups.[6]

Through the eight-week experience diverse members of the congregation will develop cross-cultural relationships and competence while learning more about biblical expectations in regard to building a healthy multiethnic church. Each week is focused on a theme and includes daily reflections on topics such as theology, history, communication, competence, and biblical reflection. At the end of each day's reflection, a few questions lead participants to journal their thoughts in preparation for discussing them with others later in small groups.

The primer is an effective tool for helping you transition your church to living color. Here are just some of the ways you can employ it toward that end: use it as

- an eight-week daily devotional for individuals
- a small-group study curriculum for the entire church
- the basis of an eight-week sermon series
- part of new-membership classes or as a required eight-week small group study for all new members;
- a required study for leadership training and development
- an eight-week series for junior high, senior high, and college students
- a requirement for undergraduate or graduate courses focused on cross-cultural competence, social justice, church planting, growth and development, church leadership, or urban missions

Whether you use the Primer, or through other such means, bringing diverse people together for meals, conversation, and understanding is critical to developing a transformational community of faith. From there, of course, the body will be much better equipped to pursue transformational work in the community. Only after you first listen and learn from the community can you hope to become one with it for the sake of transformative change.

Redemptive Possibilities

Traditionally, denominations and networks have targeted new housing developments and growing neighborhoods in which to plant new churches. While it is not wrong to do so, we should remember that communities evolve and morph over time. What today is new will someday be old. If these new housing developments lack historic anchors or fail to hold the long-term interest of those who control commercial, city, county, and state dollars, local churches and their facilities will become passé over time like the neighborhood itself. In part, this is why we so often hear the story of only a handful of people left in a formerly vibrant, dynamic church and its facility. To recognize the neighborhood has changed is to recognize that what fueled interest in the past can no longer fuel it in the future. So people move on and move out.

But think about it.

In every city, there are fixed markers that anchor stability and provide for the long-term sustainability of a community. For example, in a city like Little Rock, Arkansas, or Phoenix, Arizona, where state capitols exist, these facilities will never be moved. Similarly, universities and colleges, major hospitals, and other notable sites are likely to remain right where they are for decades, if not centuries. Therefore, when the areas surrounding such institutions have been too long neglected or fall into disrepair, city leaders mobilize to pursue revitalization. They cannot let millions, and sometime billions, of dollars of investment slip away and fail to provide for continued positive ROI (return on investment).

If your church is located in such an area, what a wonderful opportunity you have to become a significant part of the revitalization process in partnership with local businesses, government, and property owners associations (POAs) by transitioning your church to living color! Or, as part of your re:MIX, consider relocating your church or establishing another campus next to an anchor institution. Then you can bring Matthew 5:16 to life as part of measurable community transformation for the glory of God.

Communities need benevolent, Christ-centered leaders like you, and churches like yours, to help revitalize neighborhoods, repurpose facilities, and renew a sense of interest and pride in certain areas of the city. In so doing, you can demonstrate the power of redemption and fulfill the vision of Christ in Matthew 5:16 as old attitudes, property, and conditions are made new. Therefore, in addition to changed hearts, systems, and structures, values and laws must also be addressed in pursuit of community transformation.

Toward these ends, consider these questions:

- Where are the anchor institutions in your city?
- How stable are the communities around them?
- What abandoned or underutilized properties exist in close proximity to your church?

72

- Do any community practices favor one culture over another?
- How can your church encourage that these practices be replaced by others that foster fair-mindedness and impartiality?
  - How can your church develop or improve support systems within the community that give everyone equal access to opportunities for spiritual, social, and financial transformation regardless of race, class, or culture?
  - How can your church become an advocate for laws that reflect a more just and equal existence for residents in the community?

Biblical Principles of Transformation

Community engagement and transformation, like the transformation of the human heart, involves the synergistic connection of three biblical principles: faith (Gr. *pistis*) must be combined with repentance (Gr. *metanoia*) to bring about transformation (Gr. *epistophe*).[7]

Faith

By faith, we believe that not only individuals but also entire communities can be made better in spite of historic or current divisions.[8]

Read

What does the Bible say specifically about community engagement and the faith required to achieve measurable results for the glory of God?

Reflect

What light can biblical or historical stories of extraordinary faith shed on our pursuit of community engagement and transformation?

Research

What churches can you visit that are operating along spiritual, social, and financial fronts that are effecting real community transformation?

Repentance

Through repentance, we believe that not only individuals but also entire communities can be made better in spite of historic or current divisions.[9]

Admit

In every person and culture, certain opinions, traditions, and ways of thinking must be recognized as wrong before the Lord.

Acknowledge

When and where appropriate, be willing to acknowledge or ask forgiveness of diverse others for wrongs you, or those with whom you are identified, have committed.

Act

Wash the feet of those who harbor bitterness, resentment, hurt, pain, or confusion. Where possible, do this publicly as a statement of humility and of commitment to renewal.

Mosaic Church • Little Rock, Arkansas

From the Desk of Pastor Harry Li

Over the years, I've heard others questioning whether the act of foot washing really translates to our own time and culture. Did Christ intend it to be just a metaphor, or was it something he desires us to practice as well? Rather than argue for one position or another, I will simply confess that I am compelled to wash the feet of others as a concrete illustration of Christ's love.

Similar to Communion and baptism, foot washing is an outward expression of an inner reality. I have found the practice to be useful in communicating the kind of attitude we want all members to display toward one another across ethnic and economic lines, especially in times of relational struggle.[10]

Transformation

In pursuit of transformation, we see the hand of God performing miracles in the lives of people, relationships, and communities.[11]

Create

Encourage your people to financially support existing programs in the community, to partner with others already serving to meet needs, or, where necessary, start new initiatives to advance the common good.

Communicate

Encourage dialogue that breeds understanding, forgiveness, and love.

Celebrate

Promote transformative wins through public testimony and social media.

Freeman Heights (Southern Baptist Convention) • Garland, Texas

From Traditional to Transformational

Pastor Larry Venable

Historically we were a traditional church, but we didn't decide to transition to living color out of panic or desperation. In fact, we were a healthy church in so many ways; but even so, we were not impacting our changing community. Our homogeneity left us ill-equipped to deal with the advancing ethnic, economic, and cultural diversity just outside our doors. Rather than bemoan the change or seek to relocate in another area of the city, we began to ask: How can we stay in this community and become a church where every demographic group can belong? More important, we asked: What does God want us to do?

From that moment on, there could be no more "business as usual." Our new vision and mission compelled us to transition to becoming a multiethnic, economically diverse, and multisite ministry. We became intentional and began to promote a spirit of inclusion in Bible studies and in worship. For us, this meant becoming a bilingual church featuring English and Spanish in one worship experience. We began to sing in both languages and to provide translation of the messages via headsets. This brought change to our first campus, and today our formerly monocultural church family is approximately 35 percent Hispanic.

Rather than expand our existing campus, God later moved us to buy a bankrupt health club that today houses over twenty complementary ministries! Over the years we have watched Christians, churches, and people from the community serve side by side at this unique center, together impacting our community and sharing the gospel.

As of this writing, we are still in transition but continue to pursue the transformation of our church and our community for the sake of the gospel. Here are a few things we've learned.

Pursue transformation, not change.

The goal is not to make a few changes but to become an entirely different church—different in vision, mission, and makeup! A church that has transitioned to living color is uniquely poised to transform its community.[12]

Redefine your scorecard.

Jesus said if you want to be great in the kingdom of God, you must be the servant of all. A great church is determined not by the size of its buildings, attendance, or budgets. A great church reflects and serves its community, whether twenty, two hundred, or two thousand people attend on Sunday mornings.[13]

Think mission over membership.

No one wants to lose members, but not everyone wants transformation. The fact is, you are going to lose members in almost every transitional move. Remember, it is more important for the church to be on mission than it is to keep members.

Prepare new wineskins.

Traditional churches often lack missional leadership. Take the time to teach, train, and produce transformational leaders. And don't limit those you train by age or talent. It's about heart and spirit.

Operate from a mind-set of abundance, not scarcity.

In God's will is God's provision; and the gospel of Jesus is the power for change in any life, any church, and any community! Move with the Spirit and trust him to take care of everything else. To and for what he's called you, he will provide.

Be patient.

When possible, make the transition slow and sure. My image for transition is that of a road with a large boulder in the way. You can blow up the boulder, sending debris everywhere, or you can take a hammer and pound away until the boulder falls apart and the road is clear for progress.

The Three Rs of Community Development

No consideration of community engagement and transformation would be complete without a nod to the pioneering leadership of Dr. John M. Perkins.

During the turbulent civil rights struggles of the 1950s, John Perkins left Mississippi following the unjust killing of his brother by a policeman. Soon, however, John had a personal encounter with Christ that changed his purpose and direction. He returned to the violent streets of Mississippi to establish a Christian ministry of student tutoring, food-sharing co-ops, child care, nutrition programs, medical facilities, and Bible studies.[14]

Perkins's influence nurtured what came to be known as the Christian Community Development Association (www.ccda.org).

From the beginning of CCDA, Dr. Perkins, cofounder Coach Wayne Gordon, and others have promoted what have come to be known as the Three Rs of Community Development:[15] relocation, reconciliation, and redistribution.

1. **Relocation** involves living among the poor, worshipping with the poor, and in every other way welcoming the poor into your life. Ron Sider, the director of Evangelicals for Social Action, calls this "*koinonia ministry*," for "koinonia means fellowship with someone or participation in something. . . . I am thoroughly convinced, however, that the overwhelming majority of Western churches no longer understand or experience biblical koinonia to any significant degree."[16]

Examples of *relocation* include the following:

- Individuals moving to live as one with and among the poor

- Listening to their personal stories

- Visiting the poor
  o   in their first place (their homes)
  o   at their second place (their jobs)
  o   at their third place (places they socialize)[17]

- Mobilizing to meet the needs of the poor by appropriating assets (people, programs, and facilities) in impoverished areas

2. **Reconciliation** invites diverse people into a personal relationship not only with Christ but because of Christ, into personal relationships with one another beyond worldly distinctions, as we discussed more thoroughly in chapter 1. Reconciliation is a reminder that in socially and racially divided biblical times, a formerly intolerant Paul writes, "There is neither Jew nor Greek; there is neither slave nor free; nor is there male and female, for you are all one in Christ Jesus" (Gal 3:28). Dr. Martin Luther King Jr. often acknowledged that the goal of his efforts was reconciliation, redemption, and "the creation of the Beloved Community."[18]

Examples of *reconciliation* include the following:

- Two homogeneous churches representing different cultures merging to form one new church and staff of living color

- A staunch white Republican and a dyed-in-the-wool African American Democrat meeting every week for breakfast and forging a life-changing friendship over five years

- A former KKK member confessing the sin of his past before the body on the same night that an African American woman confesses her hatred for whites in humble repentance

- A Jew, a Palestinian, and an Arab, all Christ-followers, embracing and leading the church in prayer

3. **Redistribution** includes intentional acts of sharing of resources, talents, knowledge, and time with those in less-affluent cultures. According to Dr. Perkins, it is the principle of redistribution that will ultimately "break the cycle of wealth and poverty."[19]

Examples of *redistribution* include the following:

- A church of greater means sharing financially in supporting churches and ministers in underserved areas of the community

- Spending money to help underemployed or unemployed people attain gainful employment

- A wealthier church funding an urban ministry and allowing that ministry to disperse the funds as it sees appropriate[20]

- A white pastor raising some portion his or her own financial support (like a missionary) and returning this same amount of budgeted salary to the church in order to hire a nonwhite associate who might not otherwise have the means or connections to generate income in support of full- or part-time ministry

Conclusion

As church leaders, we must adjust to new realities. By transitioning your church to living color, you can expand your influence in the community and get beyond rhetoric to results for the glory of God. Toward that end, and for the sake of the gospel, we pray you will.

Conclusion

Mobilize for Change

Regarded by many as the authority on leadership and change, Dr. John P. Kotter

> is a *New York Times* best-selling author, award-winning business and management thought leader, business entrepreneur, and inspirational speaker. His ideas and books, as well as his company, Kotter International, have helped mobilize people around the world to better lead organizations and their own lives in an era of increasingly rapid change.[1]

According to *Harvard Business Review*, "Nobody understands the anatomy of organizational change better than retired Harvard Business School professor John P. Kotter."[2]

Kotter offers eight steps that are credible, reliable, and practical. Having coached hundreds of churches through various aspects of transition, we believe they can help guide you, too, through the re:MIX process.[3] With this in mind, we have adapted Kotter's steps and added applications relevant to pastors seeking to transition a church to living color.

Eight Steps for Transitioning Your Church to Living Color

1. Create a Sense of Urgency

Congregants must understand that the need exists and the time is now for transition with the future health, growth, and credibility of the church in mind.

a. Immerse yourself and your leaders in the biblical mandate of the multiethnic church.[4] It is imperative that people understand this is not about political or social correctness, but biblical correctness for the sake of the gospel.

b. Review the introduction of this book. From your own experience, and mindful of your current context, how might you articulate a sense of urgency to your members? Articulate holy intentions and clear objectives in language that can be embraced by the body you seek to influence.

c. Ask critical questions of yourself and your congregation concerning race, class, and cultural divisions in society, as well as any that might be present in the church. Consider the implications openly, humbly, respectfully, and honestly.

2. Build a Guiding Coalition

Congregants must will themselves to walk and worship God together as one in pursuit of the dream.

a. Empower diverse leaders, paid and lay, to work together as one for the sake of the gospel. Diverse others must passionately embrace and model the vision in order to lead the people with whom they have the greatest influence.

b. Accept the challenge to share the love of God with people different from the vast majority of those already attending. At the same time, you will have to inspire the congregation to do so and to adapt to changing demographics.

c. Launch small groups consisting of ethnically diverse men and women to work through *The Multi-Ethnic Christian Life Primer* as discussed in the previous chapter. Through this eight-week experience, early adopters will grow in their understanding of the biblical mandate for the multiethnic church and gain practical insight for doing life together with diverse others beyond the distinctions of this world that so often and otherwise divide.[5]

3. Form a Strategic Vision and Initiatives

Congregants must be involved in both shaping and supporting the vision.

a. Determine a period of self-evaluation culminating in a weekend retreat for guiding coalition members. Allow the Holy Spirit to be the driving force and voice for change within the church. As it is Christ's vision for the nations, let him guide and govern the decisions of those shaping the future of your church.

b. Develop a written document that clearly articulates the why and how of transition. Involve diverse members from the guiding coalition to help you draft, refine, and embrace it, or any other new directives, before you share it with the body. People must see the future clearly before they will be confident enough to work toward it.

c. Listen but do not yield to the voices that will surely arise in support of the homogeneous status quo. Sadly, many established members will find the re:MIX challenges insurmountable within the framework of their church and consequently avoid or oppose transition altogether. Press on in spite of them.

4. Enlist a Volunteer Army

Congregants must strive to walk worthy of the calling to be one in the church through the collective use of their gifts for the greater good (Eph 4:1-11).

a. Look for men and women of peace who can help you build a healthy multiethnic church (Luke 10:6). The Greek word translated "peace" is derived from the word that means "to join." It literally means a person who helps people from divergent beliefs and even warring convictions join in unity whereby oneness, peace, quietness, and rest result.[6]

b. Organize a road trip to visit a healthy multiethnic church so that leaders and members can experience diverse men and women walking, working, and worshipping God together as one in love and authenticity.

c. Use stories to help people envision the rewards of change. While studying organizational change, Scott Wilcher found that successful change is more than twice as likely to occur if you attach a story to depict the change.[7]

New Life Community Church
(Evangelical Free Church of America)
• Aurora, Colorado

A Patient Pursuit

Pastor Jeff Noble

New Life Community Church has been a lighthouse for Christ in the east Denver metro area since its founding in 1956. During its first four decades, New Life had been an Anglo church in the fast-growing and mostly white suburb of Aurora. In the late 1990s, however, things began to change. People of various nonwhite ethnicities began moving into our city in great numbers, and the church found itself at a crossroads: Do we change, relocate, or do nothing and eventually die?

It was hard for us, after nearly fifty years as a mono-ethnic church, to make the decision to reach all peoples, let alone to actually do it. At the time, there were few resources or examples of churches that had transitioned successfully. It was then that God led pastors Myung Kim (Korean) and Erik Valenzuela (Hispanic) to approach New Life about holding services in our facility, and we welcomed them.

After a short season of having a landlord/renter relationship, however, Myung, Erik, and I began gathering periodically for dinner and prayer. As our personal relationships grew, so did our trust and love for one another, and soon God prompted us to hold periodic services and events together.

Over time, God brought other ethnic pastors and fellowships into the New Life family. With each new addition, the richness and diversity of fellowship continued to grow, and ministry ideas began to flow.

Rather than being a bastion of Anglo Christians in an ocean of diversity, New Life today is a "house of prayer for all nations" (Mark 11:17 NIV). Currently 750 people attend Sunday morning English-speaking services. Of these, almost 30 percent are non-Anglo or internationals representing thirty-five different na-

84

tions. In addition, about 250 people attend six different ethnic fellowships taking place primarily on Sunday afternoons.

So, what instructive truths can help your church develop in similar fashion?

Build Relationships

Apart from prayer, this is the most important thing you can do—everything else flows from it. Pastors Ayman Armanios, George Johnson, Ken Joo, Andrew Kizito, Nelson Lopez, and Erik Valenzuela have become some of my dearest friends! When diverse leaders get to know and trust each other, members of the church will follow their example.

Be Patient

When a multiethnic vision or calling takes root in your heart, you will want to see it fulfilled as quickly as possible. Yet in transitioning a church from mono- to multiethnic, you have to be patient. As Mark DeYmaz says, "The last thing you want to do is split your church in the name of unity!" Looking back over the last ten years, I realize New Life has transitioned through the following stages:

1. From mono-ethnic to ethnic host.

2. From ethnic host to ethnic partner.

3. From ethnic partner to ethnic incubator.

4. From ethnic ministries incubator to multiethnic church.

Where is your church along this continuum?

Be Flexible

Rather than force the issue, New Life has been very flexible in relation to our ethnic fellowships. Over time, the majority of these have felt led to formally become a part of New Life, but some have not and eventually moved to another part of the city or found their own facilities. When this happens, together we thank God for the season we have had and send them off with our love, prayers, and blessings.

5. Enable Action by Removing Barriers

Congregants must develop cross-cultural relationships, competence, and accountability.

   a. Cultivate and maintain cross-cultural relationships of transparency and trust for the sake of personal growth and organizational (vision) accountability, and in order to gather open and honest feedback concerning others' perspectives.

   b. Remain committed to doing whatever it takes to cultivate an atmosphere in which every person will be represented and celebrated.

   c. Approach the cynics—those most likely affected by or to feel displaced during the transition—personally and early in the process. Share your heart and listen to them. Research has shown that unless you go to such people, they will feel left out of the process and eventually fight the change.[8] In contrast, research has shown that by going to such people you will create new networks of dialogue that can prevent polarization.[9]

6. Generate Short-Term Wins

Congregants must see progress through projects, programs, and processes that can be undertaken quickly and temporarily in order to recognize the validity and direction of a new vision.

   a. Clearly and consistently, through every available means, communicate the church's new passion and purpose to take intentional steps toward becoming a reconciling, missional, inclusive, and transformative community of faith.

   b. Invite diverse others to begin greeting at the front door, reading scripture, praying, or leading worship; demonstrate your heart's desire that the church becomes not only filled with but led by diverse Christ-centered people.

   c. Celebrate new members of diverse ethnic backgrounds who join the church by hanging flags representing their countries of origin someplace prominent in their honor. Similarly, begin to host community meals featuring ethnic-specific foods and flavors to draw attention to emerging cultures in the church or community.

7. Sustain Acceleration

Congregants must be led to maintain an attitude of faith, courage, and sacrifice through the transitional journey.

    a. Refuse to allow inconsistency or self-positioning to take root in the hearts of leaders that might stall or otherwise discourage advance of the vision.

    b. Be willing to let people go, and bless them as they do, should they lack the will to embrace transition. Keep in mind that Gideon's army was whittled to three hundred soldiers so that God alone would get the glory (Judg 7:2-8).

    c. Work hard to ensure that language is not a barrier that keeps emerging first-generation populations in your community from coming to or later remaining involved in the church.

8. Institute Change

Congregants must embrace systemic, structural change in order to move from survival to stability to sustainability in becoming a church of living color.

    a. Appoint ethnically diverse lay leaders to all governing boards and committees. Where possible, begin sharing the pulpit with a qualified teaching pastor of a different ethnicity.

    b. Develop a working document to guide your transition over the next three to five years by defining best and promising practices for multiethnic ministry in your own church's context. Set policy and procedures for maintaining gains made under your leadership.

    c. Embrace a new personality and reputation for being a church of living color. This may require a name change or addition, and perhaps a reconsideration of your logo or current palette of colors. Should you successfully transition the church, people from all walks of life and backgrounds will want not only to see and embrace, but feel the "new you." Such considerations and potential adjustments will help achieve this aim.

Kentwood Community Church (The Wesleyan Church) • Kentwood, Michigan

Incremental Intentionality

Pastor Kyle Ray

Six families founded Kentwood Community Church (KCC) in 1979 as a church plant of Berkley Hills Wesleyan Church in Grand Rapids, Michigan. Kentwood, a first-ring suburb of Grand Rapids, is a community of fifty thousand that grew essentially because of flight from the urban core and the various promises associated with suburban life. In the earliest days of the church, the surrounding community was predominantly white. But the community changed significantly over the years through refugee resettlement, an emerging African American middle class, urban poverty pushed to the suburbs due to downtown gentrification, and large-scale immigration to the area from several ethnic groups.

My wife and I arrived in Kentwood in 1999 as newlyweds, having just relocated from two hours away in Detroit. We were invited to KCC by a coworker and decided to check it out. We quickly discovered that the church was at least 99 percent white, and we were one of the few African American families in this church of over two thousand people in weekly worship attendance. The senior pastor at the time, Dr. Wayne Schmidt, met us shortly after we began attending. He shared with us that the Lord had burdened his heart about the fact that this church did not reflect the ethnic or socioeconomic diversity in the surrounding community. He wondered aloud if we might be an answer to his prayers.

Our first response was laughter. I was an automotive engineer who had no thoughts on becoming a pastor. Fast-forward sixteen years, and it is still amazing to think back over the journey of sensing a call to ministry, quitting my engineering job, attending seminary full-time, joining the staff of this predominantly white church as the outreach pastor, and eventually becoming the lead pastor of KCC in 2010. What a whirlwind! I had not only become the first African American staff person, but

88

I was and am now also pastoring a predominantly white church in a highly diverse community.

In order to be a reflection of heaven, and of our community here on earth, we have been very intentional about making incremental changes toward a transition to living color. Here are just a few of the areas in which we have chosen to focus, and some related means by which we have advanced the cause.

Worship

Ensure ethnic diversity in worship teams, do not display images of white Jesus, embrace a variety of music styles and genres, sing in multiple languages.

Education

Require staff to go through intercultural competency training, add diversity module to leadership development curriculum, provide refresher training at staff retreats, promote congregational book studies to further provide insight.

Multiplication

Be intentional in planting multiethnic churches, develop satellite campuses in ethnically diverse areas.

Fellowship

Host diversity potlucks, celebrate Hispanic Heritage month, support a Christmas in Africa celebration, recruit and place people of color in life groups.

Staffing

Post job openings in both traditional and nontraditional places to enlarge and diversify the candidate pool, share and celebrate diverse life stories in all communication avenues, make strategic hires, and appoint Hispanic and African Ministries point people.

Today KCC is a multisite church with additional campuses in Wyoming, Michigan, and Nagpur, India. The congregation is about 70 percent white. The worship experience is multiethnic and multigenerational and represents multiple socioeconomic levels. The vision of the church is to: reach all people, engage the community, awaken spiritual growth, and launch everyone into service. If you are ever in the area, you are more than welcome at our fire.

Conclusion

Today, more than ever, we need to transition existing, homogeneous churches to living color for the sake of the gospel. By creating reconciling, inclusive, missional, and transformative congregations of faith, our churches can participate in God's mission of making disciples that reflect the kingdom of God on earth as it is in heaven. Indeed, this should be our primary goal and motivation. To do so, we will have to embrace dependence and live by faith, not in ourselves but in God; not in the natural but in the supernatural, by the power of the one "who is able to do far beyond all that we could ask or imagine by his power at work within us" (Eph 3:20). Toward that end, we invite you to join the growing number of pastors and churches committing to the journey.

Notes

Introduction

1. Throughout the work, we use the term *multiethnic church* to describe congregations in which significant percentages of two or more ethnic and/ or economically diverse people groups walk, work, and worship God together—in laity and leadership—as one. We do not use the term *multiracial church* because we recognize that the Bible speaks of only one race—the human race—comprised of many ethnicities (Acts 17:26). Similarly, we use the term *homogeneous* (not *monocultural*) to describe churches in which more than 80 percent of the congregation is comprised of a single race or ethnic group. This is consistent with terminology developed by Donald A. McGavran, the father of the church growth movement. Missionaries first coined the term *church growth* to describe a movement through which the gospel would be shared cross-culturally and new believers added to the local church through evangelistic efforts outside of North America. In time, however, ministry leaders within the United States co-opted the Homogeneous Unit Principle (HUP); repurposed it as a strategy for local church planting, growth, and development; and focused on a single race or ethnic group. McGavran himself warned that such misapplication of the HUP would lead to congregations becoming "exclusive, arrogant, and racist. That danger must be resolutely combatted" (see Mark DeYmaz, *Should Pastors Accept or Reject the Homogeneous Unit Principle?* [Little Rock, AR: Mosaix Global Network, 2011], available at www.mosaix.info/ebooks). For more on applicable terminology, see www.mosaix.info/_blog/Outreach_Maga zine_Ethnic_Blends_Columns/post/Multi-what_Define_Your_Terms.

2. Bob Whitesel, *Staying Power: Why People Leave the Church Over Change (and What You Can Do About It)* (Nashville: Abingdon Press, 2003), 169–74.

3. Mark DeYmaz and Harry Li, *Leading a Healthy Multi-Ethnic Church* (Grand Rapids: Zondervan, 2010, 2013), 42–43.

1. re: Create a Reconciling Community of Faith

1. Edited from the firsthand account of Pastor Amos Gray as shared with Mark DeYmaz via e-mail, March 28, 2015.

2. As presented by and reflecting the research of Dr. Michael O. Emerson at the Mosaix 2010 National Multi-Ethnic Church Conference, San Diego, California, November 1–2, 2010.

3. Mark DeYmaz, *Building a Healthy Multi-Ethnic Church: Mandate, Commitments and Practices of a Diverse Congregation* (San Francisco: Jossey-Bass, 2007), xxiii.

4. Mark DeYmaz, "The Zimmerman Case and the Credibility of the Church on Racism," *Christian Post*, July 20, 2013.

5. Strong's Greek, loc. G2644.

6. Quoted in DeYmaz, *Should Pastors Accept or Reject the Homogeneous Unit Principle?*, introduction.

7. Chuck Swindoll, "The Problem with Pizzazz," *Christianity Today*, Spring 2011, www.christianitytoday.com/le/2011/spring/problempizzazz.html?start=1.

8. Quoted in DeYmaz, *Should Pastors Accept or Reject the Homogeneous Unit Principle?*, introduction.

9. Ibid.

10. In 2001 the United Kingdom census stirred up controversy by using the following list of ethnicities. We are reprinting them here, not to offend, but to demonstrate the challenge and fluidity of ethnic designations. White: British, White: Irish, White: Other; Mixed: White and Black Caribbean, Mixed: White and Black African, Mixed: White and Asian, Mixed: Other; Asian: Indian, Asian: Sri Lankan, Asian: Pakistani, Asian: Bangladeshi; Other: Black or Black British: Black Caribbean, Black or Black Brit-

ish: Black African, Black or Black British: Other; Chinese or Other: Chinese, Chinese or Other: Other.

11. Joseph V. Hickey and William E. Thompson have created these generally accepted socioeconomic categorizations. For more information, see Hickey and Thompson, *Society in Focus: An Introduction to Sociology* (Boston, MA: Allyn & Bacon, 2004); and David Jaffee, *Levels of Socio-Economic Development Theory* (New York: Praeger, 1998). These categorizations are described by us as follows:

- The Upper Socioeconomic Level (in North America, approximately 1–5 percent of the population) is characterized by control of economic, business, and political organizations and institutions.

- The Middle Socioeconomic Levels:

  o The Upper Middle Socioeconomic Level (in North America, approximately 15 percent of the population) represents white-collar workers who hold graduate degrees and at work have a significant degree of flexibility and autonomy.

  o The Lower Middle Socioeconomic Level (in North America, approximately 33 percent of the population) represents people who usually have some college education and are white-collar workers with a degree of flexibility and autonomy at work, but not as much as those at the Upper Middle Socioeconomic Level.

- The Lower Socioeconomic Levels:

  o The Working Socioeconomic Level (in North America, approximately 30 percent of the population) represents both white- and blue-collar workers with jobs distinguished by low job security, inadequate pay, and worries about losing health insurance.

  o The Lower Socioeconomic Level (in North America, approximately 15 percent of the population) represents people who often go through cycles of part-time and full-time jobs and often work more than one job to meet needs.

12. For more on the distinguishing characteristics of each generation, see Bob Whitesel, *Preparing for Change Reaction* (Indianapolis: Wesleyan Publishing House, 2007), 52–56; and Bob Whitesel and Kent R. Hunter, *A House Divided: Bridging the Generation Gaps in Your Church* (Nashville: Abingdon Press, 2000).

13. Annalyn Kurtz, "White kids will no longer be a majority in just a few years," CNN.com, May 15, 2013, http://money.cnn.com/2013/05/15 /news/economy/minority-majority/.

14. Rebecca Klein, "A Majority of Students Entering School This Year Are Minorities, but Most Teachers Are Still White," *HuffPost Politics* (blog), September 3, 2014, www.huffingtonpost.com/2014/09/03/student-teacher demographics_n_5738888.html.

15. Bruce Drake, "6 new findings about Millennials," Pew Research Center, March 7, 2014, www.pewresearch.org/fact-tank/2014/03/07/6 new-findings-about-millennials/.

16. "U.S. Census Bureau Projections Show a Slower Growing, Older, More Diverse Nation a Half Century from Now," U.S. Census Bureau, news release, December 12, 2012, www.census.gov/newsroom/releases /archives/population/cb12-243.html.

17. Bruce Drake, "The Civil Rights Act at 50: Racial Divides Persist on How Much Progress Has Been Made," Pew Research Fact Tank, April 9, 2014, www.pewresearch.org/fact-tank/2014/04/09/the-civil-rights-act-at -50-racial-divides-persist-on-how-much-progress-has-been-made/.

18. Scott Thumma, "Racial Diversity Increasing in U.S. Congregations," *HuffPost Religion* (blog), March 24, 2013, www.huffingtonpost.com/scott -thumma-phd/racial-diversity-increasing-in-us-congregations_b_2944470 .html.

19. John Bingham, "Churches Are Best Social Melting Pots in Modern Britain," *Telegraph (UK)*, December 7, 2014, www.telegraph.co.uk/news /religion/11276878/Churches-are-best-social-melting-pots-in-modern -Britain.html.

20. "John A Kirk," University of Arkansas at Little Rock, accessed March 4, 2016, http://ualr.edu/history/index.php/john-a-kirk/.

21. Personal e-mail from Dr. John A. Kirk to Mark DeYmaz, March 21, 2015.

22. For a more thorough exegesis of the biblical mandate for a multi-ethnic church, including Christ's Prayer, Antioch's Pattern, and Paul's Mystery as listed here, see DeYmaz, *Building a Healthy Multi-Ethnic Church*, chap. 1–3.

23. Personal e-mail to the authors, February 18, 2015.

24. For a more thorough explanation of the seven core commitments, see DeYmaz, *Building a Healthy Multi-Ethnic Church*, chap. 4–10.

25. Bob Whitesel, *The Healthy Church: Practical Ways to Strengthen a Church's Heart* (Indianapolis: Wesleyan Publishing House, 2013).

26. "Reconciliation," Christian Community Development Association, accessed March 4, 2016, www.ccda.org/about/ccd-philosophy/reconciliation.

2. M: Create a Missional Community of Faith

1. Ariane De Vogue, "Hobby Lobby Wins Contraceptive Ruling in Supreme Court," ABC News, June 30, 2014, http://abcnews.go.com/Politics/hobby-lobby-wins-contraceptive-ruling-supreme-court/story?id=24364311.

2. Mark DeYmaz, "Evangelicals and Politics: Championing Political Positions as If Written in Biblical Stone Hurting Church's Purpose," *Christian Post*, July 11, 2014, www.christianpost.com/news/evangelicals-and-politics-championing-political-positions-as-if-written-in-biblical-stone-hurting-churchs-purpose-123162/.

3. In reviewing "Steven Miller in the Age of Evangelicalism: America's Born-Again Years," Thomas Kidd suggests that Miller "doesn't work very hard to define [Evangelicalism]; he says only (in a parenthetical

aside) that evangelicalism is 'the label commonly given to the public expression of born-again Christianity.'" See Thomas Kidd, "The 'Evangelicals' Who Are Not Evangelicals," *Patheos*, July 8, 2014, www .patheos.com/blogs/anxiousbench/2014/07/the-evangelicals-who-are-not -evangelicals/#ixzz370mOZUe6.

4. According to *Wikipedia*, Christian universalism is a school of Christian theology that includes the belief in the doctrine of universal reconciliation, the view that all human beings will ultimately be restored to a right relationship with God in heaven and the New Jerusalem; see "Christian Universalism," accessed March 4, 2016, https://en.wikipedia.org/wiki /Christian_Universalism.

5. DeYmaz, "Evangelicals and Politics: Championing Political Positions as If Written in Biblical Stone Hurting Church's Purpose."

6. Neil Cole, *Church 3.0: Upgrades for the Future of the Church* (San Francisco, CA: Jossey-Bass, 2010), 106.

7. Dave Gibbons made these comments in response to a presentation made by Mark DeYmaz, and during a question-and-answer time with the audience, as part of a pre-conference panel of pastors discussing multisite churches at the Exponential Conference hosted by Saddleback Church in October 2014. Both Dave and Mark were part of the five-person panel.

8. Mark DeYmaz and Oneya Fennell Okuwobi, *The Multi-Ethnic Christian Life Primer* (Little Rock, AR: Mosaix Global Network, 2014).

9. Pastor Bob Roberts is well known for encouraging churches to embrace and pursue this mind-set. See Mark Galli, "Glocal Church Ministry," *Christianity Today*, August 2, 2007, www.christianitytoday.com/ct/2007 /july/30.42.html.

10. Michael O. Emerson, "A New Day for Multiracial Congregations," *Yale University Reflections*, April 11, 2013, http://reflections.yale.edu/arti cle/future-race/new-day-multiracial-congregations.

11. As more thoroughly discussed in DeYmaz and Li, *Leading a Healthy Multi-Ethnic Church*, 204–7.

12. Some people narrowly limit their understanding of *missional* living, thinking it means acts of kindness before conversion. But scriptures make it clear this is too narrow of an interpretation of God's eternal and all-inclusive mission. For an overview, see Bob Whitesel, *Organix: Signs of Leadership in a Changing Church* (Nashville: Abingdon Press, 2010), 9.

13. "Description of a Missional Church" *Otium Sanctum—Holy Leisure*, October 12, 2009, http://otiumsanctum.blogspot.com/2009/10 /description-of-missonal-church.html.

14. David J. Bosch, *Transforming Mission: Paradigm Shifts in the Theology of Mission* (Maryknoll, NY: Orbis, 1991), 390.

15. William H. Willimon, *Pastor: The Theology and Practice of Ordained Ministry* (Nashville: Abingdon Press, 2002), 239–40.

16. Ibid.

17. Ibid.

18. Theologian Karl Hartenstein employed the term *missio Dei* in its modern sense to contrast Karl Barth's emphasis upon God's action (the *actio Dei*). A history and overview of these terms can be found in John Flett, *The Witness of God: The Trinity, Missio Dei, Karl Barth, and the Nature of Christian Community* (Grand Rapids, MI: William B. Eerdmans Publishing, 2010).

19. Whitesel, *Organix*, 9.

20. Ibid.

21. We believe it is important to not narrowly limit an understanding of missional living to acts of service and solace before conversion. An overview of scriptures that support a broader and scripturally based view can be found in Whitesel, *Organix*, 9.

22. For more on this, see DeYmaz, *Building a Healthy Multi-Ethnic Church*, chapter 5.

23. "O, Divine Master, grant that I may not so much seek to be

consoled as to console; to be understood as to understand; to be loved as to love . . ."

24. To create, refocus, or end a ministry, see the charts in Bob Whitesel, *Cure for the Common Church: God's Plan to Restore Church Health* (Indianapolis: Wesleyan Publishing House, 2012), 42–47.

25. Dana Baker is a campus pastor at Grace Chapel in Lexington, Massachusetts. She shared these insights via personal correspondence with the authors (February 2015).

26. For examples, see chapters "Why Grow Small?" and "How Does a Church Grow Small?" in Whitesel, *Cure for the Common Church.*

27. In his book *Organix,* Bob Whitesel describes a biblical scorecard that takes into consideration cross-cultural impact. The categories from Acts 2 are:

- Measure a church's growth in spiritual maturity (Acts 2:42-43).

- Measure a church's growth in unity (Acts 2:44-46a).

- Measure a church's growth in favor among non-churchgoers (Acts 2:47b).

- Measure a church's growth in conversion (Acts 2:47c).

3. I: Create an Inclusive Community of Faith

1. Emerson's conclusions were cited by David T. Olson in a presentation delivered at Mosaix National Multi-Ethnic Church Conference in San Diego, California, November 2–3, 2010.

2. Ibid.

3. Ibid.

4. Ibid.

5. The biblical mandate for the multiethnic church and the seven core commitments required to bring it about are thoroughly discussed in DeYmaz, *Building a Healthy Multi-Ethnic Church.*

6. This statement is in fact the title of Pastor Boyd's book published in 2008 by Baker Publishing Group.

7. "Our History," The Russian Club, Ltd., accessed March 4, 2016, www.russianclubsydney.com/our-history.

8. "Rembrandt Dutch Club," accessed March 4, 2016, www.rem brandtdutchclub.com/en/sydney/home.

9. Dr. Rodney L. Cooper is the Kenneth and Jean Hansen Professor of Discipleship and Leadership Development; director of the Center for the Development of Evangelical Leadership (CDEL); director of graduate programs in counseling.

10. C. Peter Wagner, *Frontiers in Missionary Strategy* (Chicago: Moody Press, 1972), 96.

11. John Fawcett, "Blest Be the Tie That Binds," *The United Methodist Hymnal* (Nashville: United Methodist Publishing House, 1989), 557.

12. E-mail exchange between Michael O. Emerson and Mark DeYmaz, June 27, 2015.

13. "These comprehensive educational studies conclude that a racially integrated student body is necessary to obtain cross-racial understanding, which may lead to a reduction of harmful stereotypes and bias." Willis Hawley, "Cross-Racial Understanding and Reduction of Racial Prejudice," *Teaching Tolerance*, www.tolerance.org/supplement/cross-racial-understanding -and-reduction-racial-prejudice.

14. Notes from a DMin class as taught by Dr. Rodney L. Cooper at Gordon-Conwell Theological Seminary, May 2015, where he serves as the Kenneth and Jean Hansen Professor of Discipleship and Leadership Development; director of the Center for the Development of Evangelical Leadership (CDEL); and director of graduate programs in counseling.

15. See www.mosaix.info/Services/professional-services.

16. For more insights, see Charles Kraft, *Christianity in Culture: A Study of Dynamic Biblical Theologizing in Cross-Cultural Perspective* (Maryknoll,

NY: Orbis Books, 1979), 113; and Ruben G. Rumbaut, "Acculturation, Discrimination, and Ethnic Identity Among Children of Immigrants," in *Discovering Successful Pathways in Children's Development: Mixed Methods in the Study of Childhood and Family Life*, ed. Thomas S. Weisner (Chicago, IL: University of Chicago Press, 2005).

17. Organizations comprised mostly of selective adapters may be more harmonious, according to Alejandro Portes and Ruben G. Rumbaut, *Immigrant American: A Portrait* (Los Angeles, CA: University of California Press, 1996).

18. See "Five Types of Multicultural Churches" in Whitesel, *The Healthy Church*, 62–73. You'll find graphs depicting five different types of multicultural (multiethnic) churches along with the strengths and weaknesses of each.

19. Pastor Dan Backens, New Life Providence Church, Virginia Beach, Virginia, as cited in DeYmaz, *Leading a Healthy Multi-Ethnic Church*, 182–83.

20. Pastor Curtis Thompson, Key Largo, Florida, as shared with Bob Whitesel, February 21, 2014.

21. DeYmaz, *Building a Healthy Multi-Ethnic Church*, 72.

22. John M. Perkins, *A Quiet Revolution: The Christian Response to Human Need, A Strategy for Today* (Pasadena, CA: Urban Family Publications, 1976). For John Perkins's amazing story of evangelism wed with social action, see Charles Marsh and John M. Perkins, *Welcoming Justice: God's Movement Toward Beloved Community* (Downers Grove, IL: InterVarsity Press, 2009).

23. For more ideas about how to foster lifelong learning about cultural differences, see chapter 9, "Train for Change," in Whitesel, *Preparing for Change Reaction*, 173–81.

4. X: Create a Transformative Community of Faith

1. Outline of Biblical Usage created by Larry Pierce, available online via the Blue Letter Bible: www.blueletterbible.org/lang/lexicon/lexicon.cfm?bn=54&ot=KJV&strongs=G2570&t=NASB.

2. See DeYmaz, *Building a Healthy Multi-Ethnic Church*, chapter 10, where these four aims are listed and discussed additionally.

3. Gary McIntosh, "The Life and Ministry of Donald A. McGavran: A Short Overview," www.churchgrowthnetwork.com/freebies2/2015/3/13 /the-life-and-ministry-of-donald-a-mcgavran.

4. John R. W. Stott, *Christian Mission in the Modern World* (Downers Grove, IL: InterVarsity Press, 1975).

5. C. S. Lewis, *Mere Christianity* (New York: Harper One, 1952), 207.

6. Mark DeYmaz and Oneya Okuwobi, *The Multi-Ethnic Christian Life Primer* (Little Rock, AR: Mosaix, 2013), is available from Mosaix Global Network. For more information, see www.mosaix.info/workbooks /the-multi-ethnic-christian-life-primer-workbook.

7. Richard Peace, "Conflicting Understandings of Christian Conversion: A Missiological Challenge," *International Bulletin of Missionary Research* 28, no. 1 (January 2004): 8.

8. "Faith" in Greek is *pistis*, which means "faith, trust, confidence in God," which infers an inner assurance in God's purpose for humankind that leads to conversion. W. Bauer, William F. Arndt, and F. Wilbur Gingrich, *A Greek-English Lexicon of the New Testament*, 3rd. ed. (Chicago: University of Chicago Press, 2001), 668–70.

9. "Repentance" in Greek is *metanoia*, and it is oftentimes used in conjunction with *epistrophe* (see note 11 in this chapter). *Metanoia* "conveys the idea of turning, but focuses on the inner, cognitive decision to make a break with the past." Peace, "Conflicting Understandings of Christian Conversion," 8.

10. DeYmaz, *Leading a Healthy Multi-Ethnic Church*, 293.

11. *Epistrophe* is the Greek word for "conversion or transformation." It means to "turn around . . . a change of mind . . . [to turn] from something to something [else]." Bauer, Arndt, and Gingrich, *A Greek-English Lexicon of the New Testament*, 301. Richard Peace describes this helpfully

as a "reversing direction and going the opposite way." Peace, "Conflicting Understandings of Christian Conversion," 8.

12. To understand a biblical theology of change, see Whitesel, *Preparing for Change Reaction,* 75–113.

13. See note 25 in chapter 2.

14. For more on John Perkins's ideas for community development, see Marsh and Perkins, *Welcoming Justice,* and Perkins, *A Quiet Revolution.*

15. Marsh and Perkins, *Welcoming Justice,* 28–31.

16. Ron Sider, *Rich Christians in an Age of Hunger: A Biblical Study* (Downers Grove, IL: InterVarsity, 1977), 105, 193.

17. For more on first, second, and third places, see Ray Oldenburg, *The Great Good Place: Cafes, Coffee Shops, Bookstores, Bars, Hair Salons and Other Hangouts at the Heart of a Community* (New York: Marlowe & Company, 1999).

18. "The King Philosophy," The King Center, accessed March 4, 2016, www.thekingcenter.org/king-philosophy.

19. Perkins, *A Quiet Revolution,* 220.

20. Sometimes readers wonder if it is wise for a wealthier church to give money to a poorer congregation without strings attached. Because ministry must be indigenous to be successful, it is best to give with few if any strings attached. This allows learning by experience.

Conclusion

1. See Kotter International, "Who We Are," accessed March 4, 2016, www.kotterinternational.com/about-us/who-we-are/john-kotter/.

2. Editor's note to John Kotter, "Leading Change: Why Transformation Efforts Fail," *Harvard Business Review* 85, no. 1 (January 2007), https://hbr.org/2007/01/leading-change-why-transformation-efforts-fail/ar/1.

3. Ibid.

4. For a thorough discussion, see DeYmaz, *Building a Healthy Multi-Ethnic Church*, chapters 1–3.

5. For further details, see www.mosaix.info/workbooks/the-multi-eth nic-christian-life-primer-workbook#sthash.Nqc9Mfv7.dpuf.

6. James Strong, *The New Strong's Exhaustive Concordance of the Bible* (Carol Stream, IL: Thomas Nelson, 1990), 1515.

7. Scott Wilcher, "MetaSpeak: Secrets of Regenerative Leadership to Transform Your Workplace," dissertation presented at the Turnaround 2020 Conference, Nashville, Tennessee, 2013.

8. Whitesel, *Staying Power*; and Whitesel, *Preparing for Change Reaction.*

9. Bruno Dyck and Frederick A. Starke, "The Formation of Breakaway Organizations: Observations and a Process Model," *Administrative Science Quarterly* 44, no. 4 (December 1999): 792–822; and Frederick A. Starke and Bruno Dyck, "Upheavals in Congregations: The Causes and Outcomes of Splits," in *Review of Religious Research* 38, no. 2 (December 1996): 159–74.

CPSIA information can be obtained
at www.ICGtesting.com
Printed in the USA
LVOW04s1148200416

484394LV00005B/7/P